Desperately Seeking Advice

Lots of love

Sue Roberts

Desperately Seeking Advice

SUE RITTER

WORD PUBLISHING

Word (UK) Ltd
Milton Keynes, England

WORD AUSTRALIA
Kilsyth, Victoria, Australia

STRUIK CHRISTIAN BOOKS (PTY) LTD
Maitland, South Africa

JOINT DISTRIBUTORS SINGAPORE –
ALBY COMMERCIAL ENTERPRISES PTE LTD
and
CAMPUS CRUSADE

CHRISTIAN MARKETING NEW ZEALAND LTD
Havelock North, New Zealand

JENSCO LTD
Hong Kong

SALVATION BOOK CENTRE
Malaysia

DESPERATELY SEEKING ADVICE

ISBN 0-85009-596-4   (Australia ISBN 1-86258-271-8)

Scripture quotations are from The Youth Bible, New Century Version, copyright © 1991 by Word Publishing, Dallas, Texas 75039. Used by permission.

Reproduced, printed and bound in Great Britain for Word (UK) Ltd., by Cox & Wyman Ltd., Reading.

93 94 95 96 / 10 9 8 7 6 5 4 3 2 1

DEDICATED TO . . .

. . . youth leaders everywhere who have to deal with these questions every day of their lives! Haven't you always wanted to say . . . 'Here read this, it tells you what you need to know.'? I hope you will find this book a bit of a lifeline for your soul-destroying, thankless task of leading young people in your church!

Sue

Introduction

I saw this great badge once, it said 'TAKE MY ADVICE . . . I'M NOT USING IT.' Good, eh? Well, I hope I can be of a little more use than that. This book is especially for people who are thinking of becoming Christians . . . or they have just become Christians, and it's all a bit mind-blowing. There are so many things you'd love to ask, but you're not quite sure who to go to and even if you do, they might think you're really stupid for not knowing the answer. I have asked all these questions at one time or another, and over the years the answers tend to change a bit as you live your life out for Jesus, but I hope I've been honest and straight with you . . . because that's the way answers should be.

Contents

1

'I get so fed up with church!'

Dear Sue,

Can you help me? I mean, it's not like I'm a Christian or anything, I am ... but does that mean that I have to go to church all the time? I get so fed up with it!

It's the great mystery of our time isn't it? Why, oh why, do people make church so boring? I suppose part of the answer is that we are all so different. We all want different things out of the service and we all want it our way. OK, let's start with the basics. A wise man once said, 'Going to church doesn't make you a Christian, any more than living in a greenhouse makes you a tomato!' There's an element of truth in this—but don't think I'm giving you the go-ahead *not* to go to church! But maybe part of the reason church can be so boring is because Jesus isn't as real to us as we would like Him to be. Yes, I know you say you're a Christian and I believe you, but remember that He's also the best friend you've got.

I can remember having a friend I liked very much; we had a lot of laughs together and shared

11

lots of interests, but every now and then we had to have tea round at her house. Oh, what a bore! Her mum would get out the best china and cut up little sandwiches and we would all sit there looking at each other and smiling politely. It was never-ending and we were never allowed to put the TV on because that was rude when you had 'company'. I always had to wear the same dress because my mum thought it was 'neat' and so I always looked the same, sat on the edge of the same chair and had the same quiet conversation.

Then one great day I had to call round uninvited and it was a Saturday morning. Jan had left some of her school work with mine and I knew she needed it for homework so I just dashed round with it. Jan's mum answered the door in her dressing gown! Oh, it was brilliant! She looked so shocked to see me, but her good manners wouldn't allow me to stand on the doorstep so I was asked in. It was just great! The TV was blaring away in one room with no one watching it and Jan's little sister was in the middle of tipping her Weetabix onto the kitchen table. Jan herself ran down the stairs in an old sweatshirt and a pair of jeans—she had one sock on and one sock off and looked as if she'd just got up! (I found out later that she had.) There was nothing left to do but sit at the untidy kitchen table and join them in a late breakfast!

You know, after that we got on really well and the 'tea times', although still very proper, were an awful lot more fun.

Now, don't tell me you don't know what I'm getting at! When we go to church we go firstly because Jesus is a good friend to us, but after that it gets complicated. His House is holy and we want to do it justice . . . but unfortunately in doing that we often end up not being real. Our clothes aren't the ones we're comfy in, our voice tends to go all funny and sometimes a bit posh. We start smiling at everyone so that people can see how kind we are, what lovely Christians we are . . . when the real picture isn't like that. Don't you prefer people when they're being real? I'm sure Jesus does, and let's face it, we can't fool Him, can we? So part of the problem of going to church is our own attitude to it.

And just think of the poor bloke running the service! It must be so much easier to preach and convene a meeting when people are looking relaxed and happy. It's a sort of knock-on effect . . . you sit there with a false polite look on your face, so the person next to you thinks he must look the same. By the time it's gone along the whole row of seats anyone would think you were waiting to be sentenced!

You all look down at the newsletter that was given to you as you came in, and try desperately not to communicate with anyone. By the time the minister says 'good morning' the whole church has turned into a solid block of ice! The minister is now wondering what on earth he's done wrong and flounders around with bits of paper while he composes himself again.

You know what it's like when you want to tell someone something really great, and you run up and say 'Hey, guess what??!!' and they turn round with the 'who cares?' look on their face, and you end up saying, 'Oh, never mind, it wasn't important.' I think we make that atmosphere in church ourselves.

So how about sitting comfortably and smiling encouragingly at your minister? . . . you'll never know how much good you did him! And while we're rolling, let's go and talk to someone we don't normally talk to. How about someone from a different age group—different era even?? A lot of this is not so much about breaking down the boredom, as breaking down the barriers!

So there we are . . . exercise number one: wear your comfy clothes and help to put others at their ease!

The next thing you need to do is join in. Yes, join in! We both know that when someone stands up to pray it can be a long and boring process. Pretty words, clever sentences and very reverently spoken. So why do people do that? Easy! because that's how they've heard everyone else do it . . . BUT! if you were to stand up and pray, 'Lord, Ryan isn't here tonight because he's got a big exam tomorrow. Help him revise and do his best. Amen'—I wonder how long it would be before two things happened. One, someone else would follow with another simple prayer about something that mattered to them, and two, at least three people would come up to you after the meeting and say, 'It was great to hear you pray tonight. So refreshing, I wish more of our young people would do it.' Yes, I'm afraid *you* are the key to an unboring church. The more you put into it, the more you're gonna get out of it!

14

And I wonder what you mean when you say, 'Do I have to go to church *all the time*?' I certainly wouldn't advise you to be there every day of the week, that's for sure! Although I do realise how difficult it is to decide what meetings are important for you to attend, and which of them will still exist without you! Unfortunately, a lot of pressure is put upon you to go to just about everything and I know you can feel very guilty if you don't turn up. It's a bit like praying really—as soon as you miss your 'quiet time', you feel as if you're the world's greatest backslider! (Anyway, we'll deal with both of those issues later on in the book.) So, if we're going to get spiritual about it—the only meeting the Lord asks you to be at is communion! This really does bring us neatly back to your attitude towards church . . . y'see, going to church will only be a living thing to you once you've understood the basics of the gospel of Jesus Christ! And once you've really understood why Jesus died for you, you will want to go and thank Him and remember His death . . . and that's why you take communion!

OK, let's stop going round in circles and talk about you and Jesus. Perhaps there was a day in your life when you put your hand up in a meeting to say, 'Yes, I want to become a Christian' or perhaps you were at a Billy Graham Crusade or one of our concerts! Well, wherever it was, it was bound to have been quite an emotional time in your life—but it's also possible that you didn't quite understand everything that was told to you afterwards. I have a friend who went to church for years and yet he recently said to me, 'You know, I used to nod and pretend that I was a Christian just like everyone else in the youth group—but I had never actually made any kind of commitment to Christ. Oh yes, I knew it all and I could talk the right kind of language . . . but I wasn't a Christian and I knew it!'

Even more extraordinary is another friend of mine who is now a very well-known evangelist speaker, believe it or not—*he* used to go round churches and large meetings giving his testimony in front of hundreds of people and *he* wasn't a Christian either!! He was just another person who had heard it all a hundred times and been brought up to believe in God—but that didn't make him a Christian!

So it's possible that you've been doing the same thing—the problem being that it's very difficult to come out and admit it *now*! So listen, if you think you fall into this category, please do something about it! You might be able to fool your friends and the people at your church, but you'll never be able to fool God in a million years. And of course, this will be playing a major part in why you find the church so boring. If you don't know Jesus for yourself, it will be like sitting with a load of people who all know each other and all have a mutual acquaintance. It's the worst thing in the world, sitting there listening to them talking about good old 'Andy' and that time when he won the school football match by scoring the only goal— 'and hey, what about the story he told about the kangaroo?? Wasn't that the cleverest tale you'd ever heard?? And then of course, he was so kind to Sarah after the kitten incident . . . ' I can't stand 'Andy' already, can you? Well, you have to admit that you're kind of jealous because you've been left out. And that's how you're going to feel at church, when everyone's praising and singing about Someone you've never personally met.

So you need to check yourself out. If you know in your heart that church to you is just some kind of social gathering and not the place to be because you love Jesus, then admit it and sort out what you want to do about it. If you *are* in the same predicament as my friend who didn't know the Lord, then either you need to get up the courage to talk to your youth leader, minister or friend about it, or you need to tell Jesus and ask Him to be real to you.

Church will never ever be fun while you don't know the One it's all about. So please go over this chapter again and make your own decision about you and your church.

2

'I go SO red!'

Dear Sue,

My problem is that I go red very easily and I'm not finding it at all easy to tell my friends that I became a Christian recently. It seems the longer I put it off . . . the worse it gets!

Yes it does, doesn't it? So first, we have to distinguish whether you don't like the idea of telling your friends about your dynamic conversion to Christianity—OR you don't like talking to people about ANYTHING!

Happily God decided when He created us that we should all be different. Independent human beings, thin, fat, spotty, beautiful, athletic, confident, shy . . . you name it! And believe me, He wants to make something of you—but it won't necessarily be the same 'something' He'll make out of someone else!

If you are the kind of person who loves studying, writing and staying indoors, then you'll find it's unlikely that the Lord will use you as an athlete! And if you are the kind of person who is more comfortable talking to just your best friend, as opposed to a whole crowd of friends, then the Lord is more likely to use you in 'one-to-one' situations and not to witness to half the world.

Take me—I am totally happy standing on a stage talking to thousands of people, or in a classroom giving my testimony to some irate sixth-formers . . . yes, I actually find that comfortable! Now, from what you tell me, you would rather be skinned alive than witness to your crowd of friends. Well, that's fine! You see, I hate talking 'one to one'! I find it hard to sit down opposite one person and have a conversation-type chat about them and how they feel. I don't know why—I just find that harder! I do it, but it's not my favourite place to be!

You, on the other hand, would much rather be with one or just a few people—see? We're different!

I suppose one of the easiest ways to tell your friends about being a Christian, is when they ask! Because, try as hard as you might, it's pretty difficult to put 'I believe in Jesus Christ' into an everyday conversation! So, what I'm asking of you is this: when someone asks you what you did on Sunday . . . tell 'em! When someone says, 'How do you cope with such and such a situation?' . . . tell 'em! It's so much easier when someone feeds you the line. Still worried? OK, let's have a practice. You be you, and I'll be your friend.

'I go SO red!'

Friend	I left my homework right till Sunday night, did you?
You	No, I had to do it on Saturday morning. I was out last night.
Friend	Anywhere nice?
You	Church.
Friend	I didn't know you went to church.
You	You sound like a 'Head and Shoulders' advert!
Friend	*(smiles, because you haven't 'gone' for her/him)* You know what I mean! I can't imagine you in church.
You	Why? What do people who go to church look like?

(When you are asked questions about going to church or being a Christian, try to be positive in the way that you answer. Be the first one to retort with a funny line—laugh at yourself!)

Friend	I don't know. . . like 'Songs of Praise' people, y'know, all old women and opera.
You	*(laugh at description)* Gee, thanks!! I've always wanted to be able to sing like Kiwi Whatserface.
Friend	Come on, be serious, do you really believe in all that stuff?

Now let's do the conversation in the way YOU think it will go!

21

Friend	I left my homework right till Sunday night, did you?
You	No, I did it really early, then I went to church on Sunday.
Friend	Ooh! Get you! Miss Prim, so holy that you did all your homework and went to church to tell God how good you were!
You	What's wrong with that?
Friend	Trying to prove you're better than us by being holy!

You shouldn't always have to defend yourself. By taking a defensive attitude you can often offend other people, and then instead of endearing them to you, you can often be guilty of pushing them away. I think you get the idea that people are going to laugh at you or mock what you do—so before they've even started, you've taken a stance that says 'What's wrong with that?' Could you ever imagine Jesus retorting with such a daft line? It's so negative! And, as I'm sure I will say time and time again in this book, Jesus was known for what He *did*, not what He *didn't* do!!

So part of this hesitancy to tell your friends could come from a fear of what they will say and how you're going to defend it! So, Lesson One—you are the one with God on your side . . . He's rather large and doesn't need defending! Lesson Two—await your opportunity!

I'm sure you know some Christians that have the kind of charisma to go up to total strangers and say, 'Hey! Hang on a minute mate, I

wanna tell you about Jesus!' . . . and people
actually stop and let him tell them—in fact they
rather like it!! Well, that type of Christian has a
totally different type of personality from your own
(and from most of us . . . let's be fair!) and
although we all admire people who can do that, it
must also be acknowledged that it's easier to talk
to a total stranger about being a Christian, than it
is to talk to your parents, relations, best friends,
boy/girl friends. I'm not letting you off the hook—
we all have a duty to witness and if the opportunity comes our way, we feel absolutely dreadful
if we do nothing about it. Listen to these words:

> *Also pray for me . . . that when I speak,
> God will give me words so that I can tell
> the secret of the Good News without
> fear . . . Pray that when I preach the
> Good News I will speak without fear, as
> I should.*

Are these the words of some shy, self-
conscious schoolkid? Probably. But these
particular words come from Ephesians 6:19–20
and were spoken by Paul. Good old 'I've been
shipwrecked, stoned and run-out-of-town but it's
only a flesh wound' Paul!

How on earth can we not have a little bit of
fear if Paul had so much that he wrote about it??

So at least now we feel better about being
worried. But it makes me wonder what we think
God expects of us? As I said earlier, I'm not letting
you off the hook—we do have a responsibility, but
we often look at things differently.

23

A few examples: a while ago we met a Christian who had (to our minds) an incredibly interesting job. He was part of a major news programme on TV and his career sent him to all parts of the world. When John and I met him round at his house, he was preparing to go to the inauguration of President Bush in Washington, and previous to that he'd been on some fact-finding mission of NASA—I mean, this chap was busy! Later in the evening he was asking John and myself about our ministry, and living by faith, witnessing to teenagers and working in schools. We explained for a while—and then he gave a sigh and said, 'I would love to do what you do, but I'd never have the guts.' (We both gaped at him.) He went on, 'You must lead such interesting and rewarding lives—but I simply couldn't do it!'—We could hardly believe our ears! Here was a chap, going all over the world covering war-torn countries and dodging missiles, telling us that he had no guts!

I'm sure the Lord uses him no end of times . . . but he just doesn't see it.

Take my brother-in-law—another chap working for a major TV company (no relation to the first one!). Graham was always saying to us 'You know, I'm a hopeless Christian at work—I never really witness or anything.' He was finding the whole thing quite depressing, then one day we were sitting down watching TV with him and the programme was *The Cannon and Ball Show*. I commented that they seemed to have really cut down on the number of times they used the word 'Jesus' as an expletive. 'That's because I'm editing

the show now,' said Graham. I asked him how
that made the difference and he said that now he
was in charge of editing, he just cut out the word
'Jesus' every time it came up. He grinned, 'When
the producers say to me "What was wrong with
that?" I just say, "Look, I'm the editor and that
word doesn't go out on shows with my name on
them." ' Apparently the producers just shrugged
and said 'OK.'

   We were so proud of Graham, and tried to
get him to realise how brilliant that was—but he
couldn't see it, he just thought it was 'part of the
job'. Of course, now Bobby Ball is a Christian,
and maybe somewhere along the line Graham did
his bit to help him into the Kingdom!

   Once again though, it was another example
of someone not realising how the Lord was using
them. And I tend to think the same thing is
happening to you. For a kickoff, you've told me
all about it, so you're certainly not apathetic, are
you? You're worried and concerned and want to
do something about it. Here's a way round a
similar problem . . .

   Some of you will probably know that I used
to work at BBC Radio One. When I first worked
there, I was a very new Christian and not really
sure of myself . . . (Hey! I've just thought . . . I
smoked as well! Now there's a turn-up for the
books! . . .) The only thing I was sure about was
that I had found something tremendous in Jesus
and other people needed to know about it! But
how? I was in quite an intense business, with
famous groups popping in and out of the office all
the time, and as you can imagine, 'image' was

everything! The press were always on the phone wanting stories of the Radio One DJs, there were photographers on the prowl and fans waiting at the main doors. So you always had that feeling of being 'watched' and 'summed up'. As a Christian, I really wasn't sure how I should be reacting to this, so I decided one day that I should wear a 'sticker' on my then trendy denim jacket. The sticker said 'Smile! Jesus Loves You' and had one of those smiley faces you see on Acid badges now.

Anyway, I wore my sticker to work. But then as things progressed during the day, I would find there were times when I would discreetly unpeel my sticker and hide it. The first day it happened I had to go to a lunchtime press conference for some famous group (Pink Floyd, I think it was . . .) and I knew that there would be a lot of people who knew me there—so off came the sticker! Then I had to have lunch with one of the DJs so the sticker got ditched again. The third time, I had to pop down to the studio to see Noel Edmonds about something—and this time I got right up to the door, right up to the very door, and I blew it.

So after this little facade of mine, I decided there was only one thing to do—buy a patch and sew it on to my jacket. That way, I'd have to go to the extent of taking my jacket off to hide the fact that I believed in Jesus.

And it worked! It worked so well! The reason was that because I had found myself in a corner, I had to stand up for my faith. I mean, it was no real big thing this patch on my jacket—it wasn't so massive that it was all you saw, so it didn't give out 'Look out, I'm coming to preach at you.' But it did give me opportunities when people reacted to it. Things like:

> 'So doesn't Jesus love me if I frown??'
> 'How long have you been doing that?'
> 'I know someone who's into that stuff as well . . . '
> 'Does the Archbishop of Canterbury know about you? . . . Are you after his job?'

Strangely enough, I hardly ever got any negative responses and I tried always to be as nice and funny with my answers as I could. (Naturally if they wanted to talk seriously about Jesus, I had time for that too.) Earlier on we were talking about how you react to what people say—and none of the above comments should cause the hackles to rise on the back of your neck. They're merely interested questions—so answer them in an interesting way.

There's another chapter in this book that deals with ideas and ways of witnessing, so we won't go into those now, but I do want to tell you again and again that you're doing a good job and God loves the fact that you want to do more.

John was just chipping in here, when I was relating some of those stories just now, and was telling me of a Christian he knows who was a butcher. Apparently, he was really well liked amongst the customers, but his boss was always trying to cheat people. The butcher used to try and teach Kevin to put his thumb on the scales while he was weighing the meat. In other words, someone would ask for a pound of sausages and the butcher would put on an amount he knew to be less than that weight, but while he was putting the sausages on to the scales he would press the scales down with his thumb and make it look as if the weight was right. But Kevin absolutely refused to do it—he said that as a Christian he couldn't be a part of cheating people like that.

'Wow!' I said to John, 'He certainly stood his ground—what happened to him?'

John grinned at me and said, 'He got the sack!'

I must admit we both fell about laughing. I was so sure he was going to say that he now owns Tesco's or something! But what the heck? Kevin wasn't swayed from his stance as a Christian and I'm sure people would soon have found out why he got the sack—and changed butchers!

But you see, that's simply one more way where you can stand out. When your friends think it's funny to see how many Mars bars they can nick from the local shop, you don't join in. Why not? Because it's against the law!! Not just because you're a Christian! And when everyone takes the mickey out of one person in your class, you don't join in because it's unfair and you feel sorry for the person in question, not just because you're a Christian. People will soon learn that you have a more positive outlook on life and what's more, they will share their secrets with you, knowing you are genuinely concerned and that you won't tell others.

THEN, when they start to ask you why you think the way you do, you can tell them, if you think the time is right, about the God who cares for them too. There's really no need to shove the gospel down people's throats!

Before we finish this chapter, I think this little exercise would be good for you . . .

'You are what you are.'
There will always be things that you are no good at . . . things that you will make a right mess of . . . but let's concentrate on what you *can* do!

Look at this list of abilities and put a cross by all the things that don't apply to you. Then look again and put a circle round the things that you *can* do! There's a space for you to add any extras that aren't included . . .

CHARACTER	ACTIVITIES	TALENTS	INTERESTS
loud	football	music	animals
quiet	roller-skating	singing	collecting
organising	youth club	dancing	computers
making friends	athletics	drama	cooking
aggressive	Saturday job	art	crafts
shy	club member	ideas	pop music
good time-keeping	uniformed organisation	writing	reading
loyalty	charity work	public speaking	videos
laughing	aerobics group	good memory	fashion
leader	choir	maths	fishing
OTHERS	OTHERS	OTHERS	OTHERS

29

Have a good look at your list now, and see how you could help in the following situations.

1. The Christian Union meeting.
2. Your church youth meeting.
3. A large mission going on in your town.
4. The school disco.
5. The local youth club.

Start to use the assets God has given you and you'll begin to realise that witnessing for Jesus hasn't necessarily got to be an up-front thing. If you can make the posters for the mission, or you can write out invitations for a special meeting . . . maybe you could even link two video recorders together to do a quiz for the youth club? It's endless once you start . . . so start!

3

'Can I still be trendy?'

Dear Sue,

What I want to know is . . . if I become a Christian (and I'm thinking hard about it) do I have to dress differently? I get so mixed up because in my head I can only see pictures of old grannies in tweed skirts.

It would be so easy for me to say that 'God looks on the heart and not on your clothes . . .' but unfortunately people don't! I think we will always be first and foremost sized up by our outward appearance! It's funny really, when people hear the word 'Christian' they get a mental picture of what that means. Ask any kid in school and he will tell you that a Christian looks like the old lady on the TV hymn programmes. She wears an old hat, sings old hymns in an old church . . . so a Christian is definitely someone who's old. It's sad, but true, that most TV programmes with a religious flavour give this impression—I mean, they're definitely getting better, but on the whole the feeling you get is that you can't be a Christian unless you look like either an old lady or a boy scout. Following on from that, you'll probably notice that a lot of other types of programmes don't give Christians a much better deal either—look at situation comedies . . . when-ever there's a vicar in a show like that, he's always a complete berk isn't he? He's usually about 195 years old, wears a suit complete with mothballs, he's always mumbling and you get the feeling he's forgotten his own name! Actually, as I'm writing this, there's a classic advert on TV with this exact vicar driving a sporty red car down a country lane. Eric Clapton's guitar is screaming away in the background—and as the vicar drives around the bend, he's overtaken by a schoolboy on his bike!

The other picture you get of course is the token 'Christian' in just about any soap opera. Probably the best known would be Dot Cotton in *Eastenders*, the busybody with flat feet and no style who's always quoting Bible verses at everyone. In *Neighbours* we've had Mrs Mangle (the busybody with flat feet and no style . . .) to be taken over by Harold Bishop—the do-gooder who quotes Bible verses, etc. None of these characters would ever make you think, 'Gosh, I wish I was like them!' would it?

So have we got the picture everyone? A Christian is an extremely old person wearing a flowered hat, looking terrifically holy whilst casting aspersions on all around her at the same time! Does that make you feel got at? Well, it shouldn't, because believe it or not . . . we are not alone in this phenomena . . . oh no. Lots of other people go

through it too. I bet you've even done it yourself
. . . have a go:

Vegetarian: A lady with extremely long hair
parted in the middle. She wears an Indian print
skirt and a headband. Sandals or bare feet are a
must and her face is pale and spotty from lack of
certain vitamins and nutrients. She is also liable
to be carrying dried flowers and wafting incense
sticks.

Animal Rights Campaigner: A man with a long
beard, long hair and long khaki shirt hanging out
of his combat trousers. Wears a T-shirt underneath with slogan about killing off people who
wear fur coats. A balaclava hangs out of his back
pocket along with a pair of binoculars and a map
of the local college science lab. Is usually
accompanied by three or four dogs all looking
rather unkempt and underfed . . . a bit like him!

Politician: Pick a suit—any suit—as long as it
doesn't fit! Put it on an extremely fat pompous-
looking bloke, slick back the grey hair (making
sure to nearly cover the bald bit), find the most
clashingly coloured tie (what goes with grey??) and
dip the end in some very expensive soup from a
very expensive 'luncheon' with someone important.
Add a concerned but totally naive look to his face
and an ability to talk utter nonsense with a
serious tone.

The list is endless . . . and hardly any of it's
true! We just like to put people into little boxes—it

suits us to do it and somehow we feel safe like that!

But I certainly know people who are vegetarians, politicians and Animal Righters who look *nothing like* my earlier descriptions—and come to think of it . . . I know quite a few who are Christians as well!

So what's a Christian supposed to look like?

Believe it or not, there are hardly any rules and regulations to Christian Dress Sense—I think mainly because fashions and opinions change so quickly and what is acceptable today might have been totally unacceptable yesterday! It works the other way round too!

Take the case of black stockings! Ooh! Black stockings? Yes. You know, it wasn't all that long ago when a young lady would never have dared enter a church unless she was wearing black stockings along with her black dress etc. It was the only way to dress modestly. Of course today, black stockings can be taken in many different ways . . . but you'll find some in most street-walkers' wardrobes!

And blokes with long hair! I mean long flowing tresses—well, in a lot of biblical environments people would have been terribly shocked if a man cut his hair—especially if he shaved off his sideburns! Today however, older Christians don't like to see young fellas with flowing locks!

There are a huge number of ministers who would tell you they never thought they would see themselves wearing coloured shirts, casual jackets, track suits or trainers!! . . . and they've probably thrown people out for wearing them in the past! I've certainly been offered a hat from a box underneath the stairs at some churches! So what are you supposed to do?

Well, we have to dress in a way that does not outrage a sense of decency. I would tend to say that if you look in a mirror and the words coming back to you are 'provocative', 'sexy', 'tempting', then you've got it wrong. On the other hand if the words are 'fresh', 'exciting', 'enthusiastic', 'colourful', 'up to date', even 'crazy', then you have nothing to worry about. Listen, by the time someone's moaned about your fluorescent shorts and your mirror glasses—they'd be out of date anyway and you wouldn't want be seen dead in 'em!

Your main hassle is making sure that what you are wearing is not going to cause someone else to do anything stupid. Most of the time it comes down to sex. Dressing in a provocative manner sends out the wrong message and, as well as being daft, it has been proved to be dangerous too! *You know* when you're out of order, and if you look at yourself and have doubts about your Christian standards, then think again. Maybe a little 'toning down' would be in order?

Once again, no one's trying to spoil your fun and if you look around at the way God clothed flowers or patterned animal fur, then it's obvious that God has style! He put some great colours together with outrageous shapes and sizes—no two snowflakes are exactly the same . . . so why should you be?? We live in a tremendous world,

fashioned by the ultimate creator; He made these
things for us to enjoy; He gave us senses especially
to appreciate them with! So don't you dare start
letting the side down by looking drab and dull.
Even people who by their very nature are quiet can
still do the Lord justice by looking good!

Recently a lot of strange things have cropped
up at Christian conferences, things like aerobics
and Colour Me Beautiful and Stress seminars. I
was beginning to wonder what was so Christian
about these things, but in the long run if people
need to be shown how to match colours to the
colour of their hair, and if they need to keep in
shape, then it's only going to help them look good
for Jesus. Ugh, that sounds so 'New Age', but it
can't hurt to consult the experts before
rearranging your wardrobe can it? And I have to
admit that I've seen some startling changes of
appearance, especially in older people (male and
female!) as a result of these consultations . . . and
just think of it, if we can see older people learning
to cope with style and colour, it might just take the
burden off you!

I'm laughing to myself here thinking that
some of you reading this book will probably know
me and therefore realise that as far as dressing
moderately and stuff goes . . . I'm the world's
worst! Over the years, my hair has been pillar-
box red, tangerine orange, I've had beautiful
purple hair extensions down to . . . well, long
anyway! I've worn every possible colour
combination at the same time and at the moment
I'm working on a great design made out of
star-shaped silver studs for my leather jacket. It

very rarely works against me. For instance, we've been asked to play in some very exclusive private schools, based on the fact that 'You don't look like regular Christians, and we think that's good for the pupils to see.' We've been asked to loads of outreach missions, because 'You can identify with "them" and they'll understand you.'

The only time it sort of backfired on us was when we arrived at a school and played in assembly to a kind of stunned silence, only to find out later that a fifth-form boy had just been expelled for dying his hair the same colour as I happened to have mine! Whoops!

Still, it keeps people busy. At Spring Harvest (a large Christian conference) word has it that they keep a book on what colour my hair is going to be each year!! (only joking, S.H.!)

When I go shopping for clothes, I always come out of the changing room and say to John 'What do you think of this?' and he says that he can always tell if I like what I'm wearing because of the expression on my face. His answer is always the same: 'Sue, if you wear it with a smile on your face it'll look great.'

So wear what makes you happy . . . that way you'll go around with a relaxed smile and people will think 'What a nice person!' Whereas when you think people are talking about you, you tend to wear this 'I resent that, the world hates me' look on your face, and then you wonder why nobody talks to you!

So there you are. What you are is miles more important than what you wear . . . but people see what you wear first.

4

'What's going on outside my church?'

Dear Sue,

I'm very happy at my church and I have some great Christian friends. But lately, I seem to have lost touch with everything else. Should I have life outside church too?

Well, first of all it's wonderful to know that you're happy at your church . . . perhaps you can have a word with the letter writer in Chapter 1! It's also good to know that you have good Christian friends, and I'd hazard a guess at that particular fact being very much part of why your church life is happy. But enough . . . what of life outside?

There are two main dangers attached to this area: one is that people get so into the world outside that we never see them again, and the second is that they get so into the church that nobody in the world knows they exist! So somehow we have to come up with the right sort of compromise. I don't think it's that difficult a situation, but people put all sorts of pressures on you. So let's have a look at the situations and their outcomes (watch out, I feel some real-life stories coming on . . . !)

We know a bloke who is now in his thirties, who when he was young went to church with amazing regularity. This fellow (let's call him Matt) was really caught up in his Christianity—he couldn't get enough, which was fine, but along the way he was getting some unhelpful teaching. His Sunday School teacher would always remind him what a bad place the world was, and that he should keep away from it at all costs.

As Matt grew older, his youth leader spent an awful lot of time teaching him negative things. The subjects always seemed to be 'the occult', 'the evils of smoking', 'Rock music is bad for you', 'Sex is evil'. Now, it's OK to explore negative things, but the teaching on love, joy, peace, etc., was all missing. And so, Matt kept right away from 'the world', preferring to read his Bible than go out with his friends. In fact he was so busy going to church, that he had no spare time at all!

Then Matt started work. Previously there had been Christians all around him advising him how to live his life and now all of a sudden he was OUT THERE! He was at work amongst the smokers, the live-in lovers, the gamblers—and that's all he could see! His head was turned in a thousand different ways—and although he knew a lot of these things were wrong . . . he'd never been taught how to counteract it! A lot of the people he worked with were very ordinary people with families and happy home lives, but Matt could only see the bad side of it all.

So—what happened? The minute the first piece of temptation came Matt's way . . . he fell! Wallop! For all his Christian upbringing and Bible reading, when it came to reality—he couldn't handle it. It was partly his church's fault for not opening his eyes properly, and partly his own fault for cutting off his school friends who weren't Christians. How was he ever supposed to learn about the world he lived in?

Matt entered a rocky marriage which ended in divorce when once more temptation came along. He said to us one day, 'As a Christian I wrapped myself in cotton wool so that the world wouldn't harm me . . . and I was wrong, very wrong. I've made a mess of my life. I should have been aware.'

Sad story, eh? But very true. Jesus never barricaded Himself against the world. He jumped right in with both feet and survived!

Of course, if you take it to the other extreme, you can blow it just as easily. I've met so many people who become Christians, and out of sheer enthusiasm want to go straight back to where they came from to witness to their friends. I'm talking about people who have a history of drug abuse, alcoholism, prostitution etc. I mean, it's a brilliant sentiment . . . 'I know how these people feel, I can talk to them' is always the frantic reason given. It's unfortunate, but it doesn't actually work that way.

If your background has been difficult and there is no reason for you to plummet straight back into it, then you're better off learning to walk before you start to run. It stands to reason that a converted drug-addict will be able to help an unconverted addict in ways that you or I couldn't. But the temptation of the drug scene is going to be a terrible pull for quite a while . . . maybe for ever.

In the church I used to go to in the East End of London, we had a couple of blokes who felt that they would like to evangelise the pub down the road from our church. They were really enthusiastic about it and said they felt that if they were to go to the pub a couple of nights a week, and sit with the punters, they could really get somewhere with witnessing to them. Naturally, they would have to have a drink with them . . .

Our pastor was a little worried. Although he knew these two blokes to be pretty solid Christians, he had heard that they were thinking of taking a few younger Christians in with them. So, in the best way possible, he explained to them the dangers of taken young Christians back into a 'pub' type environment. In the end the two blokes went on their own, and did a good job. But afterwards I asked the pastor about it and he explained that if alcohol was a problem to you, you are best not to go anywhere near it. Then he said something which really made me sit up and listen. He said, 'If I walked into that pub and had so much as a half pint of lager . . . you'd never see me again.'

This was my pastor!! I couldn't believe my ears! But he went on to explain that he had once had a drink problem, and now he realised where his weakness was—he wasn't ever going to take chances!

I know some people would want to spiritualise that and say he should be a stronger person for being a Christian. But I know that what he said was right. It's sheer stupidity knowingly to walk into the devil's web.

Now, I'm assuming that you yourself don't have this kind of problem, but the most common way of getting in too deep is this crazy assumption that a Christian needs to come across as 'the same as everyone else'. As it happens, literally four days ago John and I were giving a training day to youth leaders in the Midlands. We were in a large church complex in Birmingham and I had just finished talking about dealing with hecklers in an open-air situation, when in walks a bloke who was obviously not supposed to be with us. I carried on talking about 'witnessing' and all of a sudden this bloke interrupts.

'What makes a Christian better than anyone else?' he said.

I answered him by saying that Christians were not 'better' but that they had seen where they were going wrong and had asked God to help them put it right. I grinned at him and said, 'By the way, what's your name?'

'Jesus,' he said.

'Hello, Jesus, I'm Sue,' I replied, realising the situation. (By this time my 'audience' were relishing seeing my training in action!!!)

'The thing is,' he continued, 'people need to

see that you are the same as everyone else . . . not better.'

'Do you honestly want me to be the same as you?' I asked him. 'Don't you wish you had a better life?'

At this he actually smiled and nodded. 'I understand what you're saying,' he said.

And it's true!! People don't want you to be like them! Most of the world are looking for better ways to live, they want love, happiness and all the things money can't buy! Ask any rich person!! Ask any successful person! They'll tell you it's not enough.

So there's no point in you leaping back into your old world with the big 'Buddy-buddy, I can laugh at dirty jokes too' routine, because your friends are looking to you for something DIFFERENT! (In case you're interested, I chatted with 'Jesus' after the meeting and it turned out he was a schizophrenic named Neil—some of the time!—and we actually had a good talk.)

So there we are, we've sorted out why you shouldn't go too far either way. And now it's time to talk about what you can do and for this I'm going to name-drop . . .

I was talking to Cliff Richard's manager Bill Latham about this very subject a while ago, and he came up with a very sensible theory. He said that he always keeps the word 'BALANCE' at the forefront of his mind. So whatever problems come up in the Christian side of things, that's the word he refers to. I think that's very sensible and I've tried it out on several occasions and found it very helpful. You see, you must make room for your non-Christian friends and family, it's very important that they see you once in a while. And there's absolutely no need for you to do anything that you would find comprising to your faith.

If your friends want to go out one night for a pizza or something . . . go with them. Have a great time, laugh enjoy yourself, enjoy the company, enjoy the food! Join in! You need to keep up with the gossip and latest news. How else are you ever going to talk to them otherwise? And at the end of the evening you haven't done anything disgraceful and your friends will have appreciated you being there. How can you possibly think of asking your friends to church if you won't even take the time to go out for a pizza with them? So you had to miss out on a church meeting—well, you shouldn't be there every night of the week.

I always say to young people, that they should have at least two nights of the week for very necessary things. The first night is to go out with your mates, or go round to their place or vice versa. The second night should be spent indoors with your family! Aagh!! Yes, and when I say indoors I mean in the same room as! Your family need to know you care, whether they are Christians or not, and the only way they are going to know is if you act on it!

Make 'em a cup of tea! Watch TV together! Be around! We'll be talking more about this in a later chapter . . . OK?

So really, the answer to your question is Yes! You should—in fact you must!—have a life outside church. And as you said before that you have great Christian friends . . . well fine, take them to the Pizza Hut next time you go!

It's a shame that this whole 'secular versus sacred' is such a problem to people. We were working at a Christian camp a few years ago where we were in charge of all the teenagers (about 700 of 'em). This was a new camp for us and we had been told to 'go ahead and do our thing', regardless of the fact that the way John and I lead a youth meeting was going to be totally different to the way the young people were used to it . . .

Well, you would have thought we had gone in there and preached some kind of heresy! You've never seen so many uptight teenagers parents/youth leaders! The backlash that we received was enormous—and we couldn't understand what was wrong! So, we sat down and went through our format.

1. A colourful backdrop with pictures of famous pop stars on it.
2. A bucket for people to write notes to us.
3. Background music as everyone came in.
4. Short seminars on the Christian life.
5. Our own techno-pop songs.
6. Question and answer sessions . . . etc. . . . etc.

So where was the problem!? Apparently, the backdrop was looked on as 'having pictures of witches behind us'. The music was evil and the seminars were encouraging the wrong sort of

behaviour! In the end we had a talk with some of
the most 'offended' to find out what they meant.
And then out it all came . . .

'We've heard that Kate Bush is a white
witch!'

'Really?' I said. 'Have you asked her?'

'Well, of course not!' they replied.

'So you don't actually know . . . ' I
murmured.

'A lot of those pop stars are into black
magic!' accused another.

'Do you know,' I began, 'that "a lot of those
pop stars" have actually started suing Christians
for saying things about them? It's called "slander"
in the law courts.'

They all went a bit quiet.

'Well, anyway,' they came back, 'you're
playing secular music in the meetings.'

'Yes, that's right,' I said. 'A lot of the kids
coming to the meetings are not Christians, they've
come with their friends and I want to help to make
them feel at ease. Playing music they know is
always helpful . . . besides, mostly it's really nice.'

'And you did a seminar where you told the
young people that you have to kiss a lot of frogs
before one of them turns into a prince!' they
complained.

We both laughed, not really knowing what
was wrong.

'Okay,' I replied. 'What do you normally do
in these meetings?'

'Well, we sing some choruses, then someone
talks to us and then we come out the front for
prayer.' they replied.

47

'That's it??' we answered, slightly shocked. 'So what kind of things do the speakers talk about?'

'The occult . . . sex . . . smoking . . . swearing . . . the evils of rock music . . . ' they answered, 'and then we go out for him to pray for us if we are doing any of these things.'

We were gobsmacked! For years the only teaching this youth group had had was entirely negative! 'You must not do this . . . you must not do that . . . ' How awful! So their lives were eaten up with all these evil things that they mustn't go near! And we had been giving them a programme of teaching about the positive side, the fun and enthusiasm side. We had been saying that it was OK to actually GO OUT with someone! We had been encouraging them to bring their non-Christian friends along as the meetings were fun!

We had been laughing and sharing about the things God puts you through in order to make you grow stronger, and what a mess we sometimes get in, but isn't it great that the Lord is watching our every move . . . and He's there encouraging us to get up and try again!

These kids obviously thought that God was watching over them with a large stick! And that everything but breathing and singing choruses was wrong!

We did actually get the problem sorted out and we had a great week . . . but the thing I really wanted to tell you about was this . . .

John and I had been watching these young kids and they had a really weird system (not all of them naturally, but a great many of them). The girls would walk across to our Youth Tent, stand outside and put on head scarves or berets and then wander in. The boys would wait outside the tent, straighten their clothes etc., and walk in. After the meeting, however, we watched the same people take off the head scarves etc., stroll away from the tent, along the field to the back of another tent and light up cigarettes! Then the snogging would start in earnest! These were the same kids! Their language was foul, their attitude was totally unchristian and it took us a while to sort out what had gone wrong.

You see, these kids lived in two worlds. When they were in the Youth Tent with us they were Christians, and when they left the meeting, they also left their Christian lives behind. They then crossed over the field to where the 'world' was. The teaching had been so negative that they couldn't handle the pressure of being the perfect Christian all the time. If your Christian life is a mass of 'DON'TS' then you are going to wind up in trouble. These kids needed to learn the magic word BALANCE! You *have* to learn to live in this world all the time! You are no good to your friends who don't know Jesus, if you can't talk to them about everyday things. This shouldn't be a problem—it's quite possible to know what's going on in *Neighbours* and still hold on to your Christian faith! You should be able to talk to someone who's smoking, without having to smoke yourself.

My friend Joy said that her parents had a very cunning way of getting her to work out the wrongs and rights.

49

'If I said to them, "I'm off to a disco with my friends, we won't be late," they would smile and say, "Fine." And then just as I was going out of the door, they would say, "Oh, by the way, Joy . . . take Jesus with you." '

Clever, eh? So Joy would go and enjoy having a dance with her friends, but she couldn't forget the fact the Jesus was watching her having a good time. She was aware of His presence . . . even at a disco! I think this is very good advice, and if you take it then I don't think you'll stray too far—and when you do (and we all mess things up) you will want to put it right, and that's important.

God gave you a conscience. You *know* when you're doing something wrong, so I don't think you can blame everything on the evils of this world. Take Jesus with you into your world, your family, your friends, your school or work. Make time for these people—they're important to Jesus and they should be important to you. GET THE BALANCE RIGHT!

5

'Won't somebody make the Bible interesting?'

> Dear Sue,
>
> I have tried, I have really tried to read my Bible! I know it might sound daft, but I find it so difficult to understand. I've lived in a town all my life—and such a lot of the Bible seems to deal with sheep and goats and corn and things. Help please!

Sheep and goats, eh? Well, I guess we can all relate to that one . . . but let's start at the beginning. Which, I might add, is a very bad place to start if you want to get anything out of reading your Bible! I've met many people who have this brilliant plan actually to read through the Bible in two months or something, and although that might get you into the Guinness Book of Records, it certainly won't help you understand anything you've read.

You see, reading the Bible isn't something you do as a challenge so that you can boast to your friends. There is nothing admirable in having read the whole Bible thirty times if it hasn't meant anything to you. I promise you it won't make you any more 'super-spiritual' than you already are! Anyway, as I was saying, the worst place to start to read the Bible is at the beginning. To try and wade through Genesis, with all its long-worded kings and funny-named places, is liable to put you off for life.

NOW! Reading the Bible from the start of the New Testament is a much better idea! Turn to Matthew chapter one and see what I mean . . . AAAGGHH! Sorry, that doesn't really help either, does it?? OK, let's cheat and start at verse 18. In my Bible this is entitled 'The birth of Jesus'. Whew, that's better, familiar ground. How much? Well, let's say today we read to the end of the chapter, which is eight verses. Now, that's not going to kill you, is it? But it's plenty if you sit down and read it properly. There's a lot in those eight verses . . . put yourself in their place—what would you have done? Verse 19 says that Joseph had it in mind to divorce Mary! Think on that for a while!

Tomorrow maybe you can read a bit more. I usually read a paragraph or even two if it's a good bit. As I said, it's not a competition to see who can read the most. In fact, if you want to turn it into a competition, then let's see who can use what they've read to the greatest advantage! Because the whole idea of reading your Bible is to act on it, one way or another. Sometimes you might find that something you've read will actually come into everyday conversation. For example:

'Did you read in the papers today that that

millionairess is expecting? They reckon the bloke
responsible is going to do a runner!'

'Really? Well, I suppose it's a first reaction
. . . I mean, even Joseph was gonna leave Mary
when he found out about her!'

Ooh, now we've really put the cat among the
pigeons . . .

Sometimes the Lord uses your Bible reading
to talk to you very directly about something that
may be bothering you. Perhaps there's something
you were worried about doing, something that you
felt you should do, but hadn't the guts to do
anything about. And then you read these words
. . . 'An angel of the Lord appeared to him in a
dream and said, "Do not be afraid." ' And
although you've heard those words every
Christmas since you were born, today it's as if
you've read, 'And the angel of the Lord said, 'DO
NOT BE AFRAID! !'

Phew! God can talk to you like that. It may
not happen every day, but when God does need to
tell you something, you need to be ready . . . and if
you haven't read your Bible you might miss out on
something important for your own life—let alone
someone else's! On reflection, I would say that
some of you reading this book today will have
heard God speak to them through that passage as
you read it just now. So get some method into your
Bible reading . . . don't just open it at random, it's
not a lucky dip. Get yourself organised and set
goals you can reach. Eight verses a day, a
paragraph every two days . . . a single verse before
you turn out the light! I don't care what it is, I

just care that we (yes, you and me . . .) read something!

All right, let's look at some different ways of reading your Bible. By the way, what version have you got? Have a real good look around your Christian bookshop: there are some great 'Student Bibles' and there's a 'Youth Bible'—these particular ones will give you a bit more insight on what you're reading. For instance, I've had a quick look at Matthew 2 and my Youth Bible has a little box at the side that says that the 'three kings' were probably neither three nor kings! Apparently the 'three' bit comes from the fact that there were three gifts . . . gold, frankincense and myrrh! Ha! Personally, I like little bits like that . . . and for all you 'townies' out there, you'll find they explain lots of the 'sheep/goats/corn' bits too!

So, what were we talking about? Ah yes! Finding different ways to read your Bible . . .

Well, I particularly like to read the letters. (You know, the ones that Paul wrote near the back of the Bible.) 'Cos if you read them as actual letters, they become amazingly interesting. I've been reading Timothy as my daily (cough, cough, splutter, splutter . . . two-daily . . . three-daily whatever . . .) reading just lately, and again I've been using a Bible with little boxes of interesting, not to mention amusing, facts on the side. Here's a great one—when Paul wrote to Timothy, he went on a bit about how training the body is of some use, but serving God helps you in every way. Well, apparently the Greek word for 'training' is the same as the word for 'gymnastics' . . . and the word for 'gymnastics' comes from the word 'nude'(!). It's a fact that in those days, athletes worked out in the nuddy! How about that? And you thought the Bible was boring!!

Anyway, as I said, I was reading through Timothy and it's a really nice book to read because it's full of encouraging things, including those wonderful words, 'Don't let anyone treat you as unimportant because you are young.' Isn't it great to know that Paul knew how it felt, so he wrote to this young bloke Tim to encourage him?

Now, say Paul had written to you . . . yes you! How would you feel? Well, that's part of what it's all about. Paul *has* written to you, and you can treat his letter as if it just came through the box and landed on the mat. John and I have actually done this for real. (Yes, I know we're crazy—but it really helped.) John went outside our house with a Bible and pushed it through the letterbox and then came through the back door and said 'Hi! I'm home, any mail?' And then we went to the front door and picked the Bible off the floor. We role-played the whole thing, from trying to guess who it was from, to opening it and reading it to each other.

Once you make something that personal, it really takes on a living image. Paul adds great lines like, 'I hope I can come and see you soon,' so it really sounds like a letter—and because it sounds so real . . . you can answer it! Have you ever thought of doing that??

> Dear Paul,
> Thanks for your letter. It was great to
> hear from you, especially as a lot of

*people have been getting at me lately
and I think part of it really is because
they think I'm too young. But I'm only
trying to put into practice what the Lord
has told me to do. And when you said
I'd be made strong by the words of faith
and teaching, I wondered what you
meant for a minute, but then I
remembered using what I'd read in a
situation at school—and it worked
brilliantly!*

Love, Me.

Why should the Bible be boring? Hey, and if
you think it's that bad, why not try re-writing it??
I've had a lot of fun with this one. It's something
you can do with a group of friends or on your own,
but it's a mega-way of finding out if you've actually
understood what you've read. If you can't put it
into your own words, you've probably not got to
grips with it.

My dad got to grips with Christianity at the
wonderfully young age of 72! And one day I was
explaining to him that I had actually re-written the
whole of one of the letters, in an effort to
understand it. He thought it was a brilliant idea,
and as a writer himself he saw it as a great way to
learn.

My husband John is a minister as well as
playing with me in the electro-band Keep In Step,
and one day he got me to read the Bible in a
service we were taking, and then I had to re-read it
how I saw it. Most of the congregation loved it . . .

most of them . . . The reading was Isaiah 55:1. It reads like this:

> All you who are thirsty,
>   come and drink.
> Those of you who do not
>   have money,
>   come, buy and eat!

However, the cockney version went something like this:

> 'Oi, come over 'ere a minute! Come and
> wet yer whistle! And you who 'haven't
> got no ackers, come and stuff yer face!'

Yes, it does actually mean the same. It's almost a market cry, isn't it? The kind of thing that Del Boy from *Only Fools and Horses* would use. But that was it! That was the message! You don't need money to buy what the Lord has for you . . it's yours, take it!

Another thing I have often done in a service, that sometimes causes a bit of consternation, is this: my pastor always said that if you were called upon to read the Bible in a church service, and you hadn't had time to read it beforehand—there was one golden rule that got you out of trouble. That was, 'Whenever you come across an awkward name or name of a place that's impossible to pronounce, just say "wheelbarrow"! It gets you out of no end of a mess.' Obviously, I do tell the congregation that this is what I was taught, but I do also actually use the word 'wheelbarrow' in place of difficult names, now and again!

The reaction is twofold. There are people that just can't take it, and think it's terribly irreverent. These people usually account for less than 1% of the congregation. And then there's everyone else, who comes up and says 'That was really great, I always get stuck on that name as well!' Personally, I think it's helped a great many people to go ahead and read out loud, when perhaps they would normally have shied away.

The other thing that people sometimes find helpful are reading plans and daily notes. But before we talk about them, perhaps we should just mention 'doing things out of duty'. With the best will in the world, we all plan to read our Bibles every day at some horrendous time in the morning when we are going to have our 'quality time' with God. Whoever invented that saying 'quality time' should be shot! It gives you the feeling that, 'This is it! The only time of day that God going to talk to you, the only moment in time when the Lord is remotely interested in you.' Which of course is rubbish. Let me tell you in big capital letters that GOD IS INTERESTED IN YOU WHETHER YOU REMEMBERED TO READ YOUR BIBLE OR NOT!! OK??

One of the worst hang-ups we get as Christians is that if we fail, we think God loses interest in us. There's a chapter further on dealing with just this one subject, because so many people get hung up on it. But for now, let's just say that, 'Once you make something a law or a rule, you lose your freedom.' In other words, it's good to have a special time that you keep for reading your Bible, but if you miss out on it, you have no right to feel guilty. God has not deserted you, He's not frowning on you from a great height—He understands the human side of us . . . He made us that way. If your Bible-reading times become a chore, then they're not worth it.

Right! Daily Reading books . . . There are many to choose from, some very general, some especially for whatever age you are. They are helpful and full of explanations and sometimes include questionnaires and things. Trouble is, a lot of them have dates and things on. So, if you miss a day, you feel honour bound to try and catch up . . . and if you miss a week!!! Well, that's it folks . . . you're gonna be reading for ever!

So you need to make sure you use them properly. Most of them really take the form of a short Bible study, so you need to make sure you're the kind of person that can handle studying as well as reading.

I've given you lots of ideas here, and hopefully you'll come up with even better ones to suit you. The main thing is that you find a way of reading your Bible that suits you. Don't treat it as something you must do, or it will end up being a drag—like homework. I know it's hard sometimes to have the enthusiasm to read—especially if you're not the reading type—so go easy on how much you do. Remember, a paragraph can speak volumes and can really change your life, and that's what it's all about. If reading the Bible doesn't change your life, then you're just 'reading the Bible' . . . you might as well read a history book.

Listen to these words from 1 John 1:1–2,4:

'We write to you now about what has
always existed, which we have heard,
we have seen with our own eyes, we
have looked at, and we have touched
with our hands. We write to you about
the Word that gives life. He who gives
life was shown to us. We saw him and
can give proof about it . . . We write this
to you so you can be full of joy with us.

Not many history books take it that far!

It's good to chat to you about Bible reading, because I always find it so much better to read little bits. I used to feel very unspiritual when people would tell me of the volumes they'd read. But when I look back to where some of them are now, I realise that they were just 'reading' . . . And I don't want that to happen to you.

So don't worry about the sheep and the goats and the corn. If you read little at a time, the Lord will say whatever He wants to say and you'll understand it perfectly. Your Bible reading is for you and you alone, and even if you're reading the same passage as the man next door, the Lord will apply it in different ways. It doesn't matter what time of day or night you read it, or whether it's at a different time every day. The main thing is that you're comfortable and you want to read your paragraph, and then apply it however you feel God is telling you.

That's what the living Bible is all about. OK?

6

'Today I tried to pray . . .'

Dear Sue,

Today I tried to pray and it felt like knocking my head on a brick wall! It's not supposed to be like this, is it?

No . . . but it often is!! In one way it's a difficult subject, prayer. I mean we all know it's just us talking to God and as such that should make it incredibly simple. But I suppose most of us are used to seeing the person we're talking to and hearing them respond . . . and when you put it like that—prayer isn't simple because we can't physically SEE God and we don't often physically HEAR Him either.

So what are we doing to do? For a start we can avoid the pitfalls that I talked about earlier in the problem with reading your Bible. Once we start making it a little law ('I must pray at 7 o'clock in the morning every day and again at night before I sleep' . . . etc. . . . etc. . . .) then we feel totally awful if we miss a go. And anyway, prayer shouldn't be something that we just do out of a

61

sense of duty . . . it should be something we do
'cos we like it! We want to talk to Jesus because
we've got things to tell Him, we've got amazing
secrets that we are no way on earth going to tell
anyone else, and of course every now and then we
get caught up by how much He loved us when we
didn't care very much about Him. On a brilliantly
hot summer's day we want to say 'Thanks Lord for
making the sun!' and on a hideously freezing
cold snowy day we want to say 'Lord, what on
earth did you make snow for?' . . . Does this sound
like your prayer time?? OK? OK, let's sort it
out . . .

The Bible talks a lot about 'praying
constantly'. How's that possible? If you take it
literally, you'd never talk to anyone else and you'd
never get anything done! On the other hand if you
look at it in a slightly different way . . . how about
'praying whenever you want to throughout the
day'. Yes, that sounds more like it! Life is so
much easier if you pray about things when you
think of them, or when you're reminded of them,
rather than trying to save it all up for your special
'quiet time'. More often that not, if you do save
it—you've forgotten what it was you were going to
pray about anyway!

People constantly say to me, 'Oh could you
remember to pray for me at 4.00 p.m. today, I'm
going for an interview . . . ' or maybe, 'Don't forget
to pray for Claire in hospital will you? . . . '
Basically, YES! I will nearly always forget, so I
tend to pray for whatever it is immediately! This
system works well for a number of reasons:

1. I've remembered and so the prayer is offered.
2. I don't have to try and remember it later tonight.
3. At the actual moment someone is telling you about a certain situation, it's an awful lot more real than it will be later on.

So everybody wins! Of course, this doesn't mean that you don't have to have a quiet time as well . . . but it does help you to keep in contact with the Lord in everyday situations, and because of that, Jesus all of a sudden becomes more real to you. He's not just someone you remember when you go to bed and before you get up—He's someone who really is with you all day.

If you still feel you need a 'system' to help you during your times with Jesus, then I still thinks the A.C.T.S. one is the best. The idea is that you think of the book of ACTS and then you have different types of prayer for each of the letters. Like this:

A. Adoration   Always begin your personal prayer time by telling Jesus how much you admire Him. As your Creator, Saviour, Healer and Coming King, He's done a lot for you to praise Him for.

C. Confess	Get it off your chest! Tell the Lord of all the things you've done wrong that day. Whether you are in the right or the wrong is irrelevant . . . don't make excuses, just confess your sins, guilt and fears to Jesus and start feeling better immediately!
T. Thanksgiving	Now that you're feeling better, you will want to thank the Lord for all the things that have gone right for you today—all those little incidents that have added up to something good.
S. Shopping List!	(Actually, the real word is 'supplication' . . . but who knows what that means!?) Anyway, this is your list of things you want to ask God's help with—all the things you know you can't do on your own. This part usually takes the longest because we need help with just about everything!

Now, if you start using this 'system' I know it will help. Try taking a letter and praying for ONE

MINUTE . . . yes, ONE MINUTE . . . if you're not used to praying for ages, then this is the best thing to do. OK, now go on to the next letter and use up your minute again. I guarantee you will need at least two minutes by the time you come to S. And then before you know it—you've been praying for FIVE SOLID MINUTES! Great, eh?

I know, I know, you've read about these 'prayer warriors' who pray up mountains—for weeks on end—and people at your church who have a 'ministry' in prayer . . . but don't worry about that! This is me and you and everyday life we're talking about! So give this system a try. I'm sure you will feel the benefit. (And like all good exercises, you can gradually increase the minutes . . . but not too quickly.)

The other thing I need to say is . . . 'Be real!' There's nothing so pathetic as trying to be 'nice' to God when really you feel like blowing the world up. What is the point of feeling all wound up inside and actually trying to convince God you're happy?

> *Dear Lord,*
> *I lost my temper today. And as you know, Brent is really a nice fella and he didn't deserve my fury. I actually like him quite a bit, so the fact that he's better than me at everything doesn't come into it. That's the way you made him Lord, and I'm quite content being me.*

True or False?? OK, here's the real version . . .

Dear Lord,
You saw what happened today—I'm
only amazed that Brent has still got a
mouth to talk with! Lord, you have to
help me because if you don't, I won't be
responsible for my actions tomorrow,
OK? What I don't understand is how
come you make some people good-
looking and others ordinary like me?
What's so great about him anyway?

Talking to the Lord like the second prayer
will gradually bring you to a place where this
happens . . .

Lord, it's not that I'm not grateful for
who you made me, and maybe if I was
handsome I'd be really arrogant—I
don't know. You loved me enough to
die for me, so you must think I'm pretty
special anyway . . . Yes, I know Lord,
I'm just having a moan, aren't I?
Actually, I heard that Brent's parents
are on the verge of splitting up—so
maybe he gets a bit mouthy because
he's frightened of what might happen.
Lord, I pray you will look after him, it
must be really horrible to be in that
situation . . .

Before you know it, that whole prayer has
turned round and Jesus has started to point you
in the right direction. I know this happens
because I've done it hundreds of times. Jesus has

a great way of showing you yourself. That's why the Bible is often referred to as 'a mirror', because once the Lord starts talking to you, you see yourself and the situation as it really is.

Up to now, we've been chatting about prayer in its usual form of you sitting on your bed or on the floor/in the loo (often the only 'quiet' place in the house!) and just praying in the normal way. But there are an awful lot more ways to pray than that! So here are some ideas that can be linked into your youth group or done with your friends—these are a lot of fun and very 'active' too!

The Market Place Prayer . . . Get together and think of famous people who are Christians. They can be pop stars like Cliff and U2, they can be athletes like Carl Lewis and Kris Akabusi, or maybe personalities like Simon Mayo the DJ or Ian McCaskill the weatherman. When you've thought of about six or eight, make small banners with their names on.

Then get the same number of people to hold the banners up high in different parts of the room. Now, like in a market place they have to start shouting out the name of the person on the banner, e.g. 'Simon Mayo! Come and pray for Simon Mayo, he needs your prayers! He's in a prominent place in the media and he needs your support!' Everyone else in the hall has to decide who they want to pray for and run over to that banner.

When everyone is gathered in groups, you have two minutes to pray with each other for that personality—then it's all systems change and off you go again! You can repeat this as many times as you have banners, to give everyone a chance to pray. And the great thing is—these people *really do* need your prayers! You can boost their Christian witness by doing this for them, and I know they will be grateful.

Magazine Prayers . . . Most churches have an excess of Christian magazines left over from sale. The idea for this prayer time is to take all the pages out of the magazines and spread them all over the floor. You need enough to cover the floor entirely . . . it looks really great when it's done.

Then you all need to go on your hands and knees and crawl across the magazine pages looking for something interesting to pray for! Get your youth leader to time a minute for you all to find something—and then a minute to pray for that article. (It could be a missionary story letter on the problem page/an advert for Christian workers . . . anything really!)

Once you have done this three or four times, you can then have great fun squashing all the paper into a big pile and burying your youth leader! (Yes, I thought you'd like that bit . . . !)

Prayer in the Air! . . . Cut lots of plain paper into small strips (about two inches by half an inch). Give these out to everyone and ask them to take their time and write something on the paper that they would like someone else to pray about. There's no need to write your name on the paper as no one needs to know who you are. Also, you might just want to put something like 'problems at school' or 'smoking', rather than the whole history!

When everyone has written something, you get to the exciting bits. Everyone has to roll their piece of paper up into a tiny 'cigarette shape' (sorry, couldn't think of another description!) and then insert the piece of paper into a deflated balloon. Ah! sorry, forgot to mention the balloons— it's best to keep them a secret until this time . . .

Once your piece of paper is safely secured inside the balloon, you blow it up and tie it. You should now have an inflated balloon in which you can see your piece of paper. If you happen to have some music handy, now's the time to play a chart hit whilst you all bat the balloons around the room, keeping them in the air all the time, but making sure they get thoroughly mixed up. Then after a countdown of from ten to one, grab a balloon, burst it and read the message. You now have two minutes to pray for whatever is on the piece of paper in front of you!

Try these things out if you get a chance, and your prayer life will never be the same again! And I'm sure that you can come up with some much better ones as well!

You see, there's no reason why prayer shouldn't be active . . . and although in one way the same prayers would be answered if you were to sit down in one place all night, it's a lot more fun to throw yourself into it and experience prayer in a different way!

7

'I seem to fancy everyone I see!'

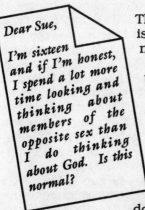

Dear Sue,

I'm sixteen and if I'm honest, I spend a lot more time looking and thinking about members of the opposite sex than I do thinking about God. Is this normal?

The quick answer of course is, 'Yes! Of course you are normal!'

But I think we ought to go into it with a bit more detail than that, don't you? There are so many questions to be asked . . . and I don't suppose you're always getting satisfactory answers. When people ask, 'Why shouldn't I do this?' I always think it's unfair to say 'Because God said you can't' . . . I mean, it's not much of an answer really, is it? If you can't do something, then there must be a reason for it. I don't think God made up rules and guidelines just for the fun of it.

Recently, John and I have been asked to go into schools and talk to fifth years. The subject we have been given is titled 'Sex, Marriage and

Abortion'. We were most upset that none of the teachers seemed to think that the word 'Love' should be included. I am a great believer in romance and find it a crying shame that so many people are advised that there is no such thing as love, or looking at someone across a crowded room and all that.

I would be very unhappy if there was no romance in my life with John. It doesn't have to be extremely soppy . . . John doesn't buy me roses every day . . . but we do enjoy doing stupid things that are going to make the other person happy. My birthday card from John will always have an extremely cute fluffy kitten on the front—'cos I love animals, especially baby ones. I will spend half my birthday money on John, because I'll always find something at the shops that would look great on him! It's all very silly but it makes us laugh, and as we don't earn a lot of money we can get a great kick out of inexpensive fun! And you see, we are not doing these things because the Bible says that a husband and wife should love each other— we're doing them because we want to!

People often say that you can 'learn' to love someone, or you can 'work' at a relationship. I think this is a bit of a myth really. Sure, you could eventually learn to love the person you married, but I wouldn't like to be around when your eyes do meet the person you really click with! So for me, romance has an important place in a relationship.

There are some terrific love stories in the Bible. My favourite is the story of Jacob and Rachel. If you haven't read it, you'll find it in

Genesis 29. It's a brilliant story of a man who saw the girl of his dreams and asked for her hand in marriage. Her father made a bargain with him: if he would work for him for seven years, *then* he could marry Rachel. Seven years! You can't tell me it's not romantic to wait seven years for the one you love.

Of course, things don't go smoothly for Jacob and he ends up being tricked into marrying the wrong girl. He finds himself married to Leah, Rachel's ugly sister. There are so many morals in this story. Rachel's sister fancied Jacob anyway, so she was dead chuffed when she married him, but Jacob didn't feel anything for her at all. And this is where the 'myth' I was talking about earlier came in.

Leah had this daft idea that she could get Jacob to love her eventually. When she found it didn't work, she became pregnant. Her reaction to this was, 'Surely my husband will love me now.' But he didn't . . . *he loved Rachel!*

That's the way it works! Love cannot be turned on and off like a light—you've either got it, or you haven't. So this is a good time for me to have a word with you about getting pregnant. This is good advice for girls and fellas alike. 'Getting pregnant will not get you your man!' A lot of boys are guilty of saying to their girlfriends, 'If you really loved me, you would sleep with me.' And girls are guilty of actually believing this line. A boy can be trying to be clever by throwing this reason at his girlfriend—but how many times have you heard girls say, 'So I slept with him, and now he's tossed me aside and told me I was cheap!'?

It's a no-win situation. Bigger trouble comes along when the girl thinks, 'Oh no, how can I keep my boyfriend? I already sleep with him and yet I think he might be going off me!' So they play the Leah game and get pregnant purposely as a way of keeping hold of the person they think they love. 'I'm expecting our baby so now you have to stay with me and we'll get married . . . '

This of course is a big joke—normally you don't see the boy for dust, and even if you get lucky and he marries you, he'll be marrying you out of a sense of duty . . . nothing to do with love. And then you're both lumbered with each other . . . until your eyes meet someone else across a room, etc., etc., and then your heartache *really* starts!

It's a mess isn't it? It doesn't work that way. Leah went on to have many children and Jacob never ever loved her, and as soon as he had the chance, he was out of that marriage and marrying Rachel.

Funny really, it's one of the oldest tricks in the book, so old that it's in *the* book! We often think that all these types of love-relationship hassles are new . . .but if problem pages had been around in Old Testament times, the letters would have been no different to today's, would they?

Anyway, getting back to your original question. God made you with all the feelings and emotions you now have, and He designed you so that by the time you hit your teens you would start to discover the opposite sex. It's funny to think that God actually invented sex, isn't it? I'm sure at times we think that we actually thought it up all be ourselves! When we were in our fifth-form lesson, we wanted the young people to ask us any questions they liked. To make it easier for them, we gave them all pens and paper, let them discuss with each other what they wanted to say, and then John went round the classroom with a bin and asked everyone to put their question in, unsigned.

We thought we would be asked some really difficult, if not totally embarrassing questions—but there were very few. I think the reason behind this was because we let the questions be anonymous. Believe it or not, by far the most popular question was: 'HOW DO I KNOW WHEN IT'S LOVE?' 'HOW DO YOU KNOW WHEN YOU'VE MET THE RIGHT PERSON?'

We were so pleased that this mattered to them. In fact, after the lesson one of the teachers found a piece of paper screwed up on the floor and after she had read it, she came over to us and said, 'I think you might like to read this. It's from a girl who I would never have thought would write it.' The note had been written to her friend and it said, 'You can tell that Sue loves John by the way she looks at him.'

You see, 'love' was still the most important factor to them. SO, HOW DO YOU KNOW WHEN YOU'VE MET YOUR MATCH?? Happily, as Christians we have much more of a chance of getting things right, because we have Jesus guiding our lives. A lot depends on how much we let Him take control. Don't worry, I'm not about to tell you that you can't go out with anyone until you've met the person you're going to marry!

Everything keeps going back to the fact that when the Lord gives us guidelines, He gives them to us for a purpose. He's not trying to spoil our fun, He's just giving us the plan of the best way to live our lives. So if you want to end up with the right partner for the rest of your life . . . follow the rules!

There could be someone out there especially for you, ideally suited for you. Someone with a similar outlook on life, the same type of sense of humour and a personality that you'll love to live with. So it's really worth praying about, don't you think?

Of course not everyone marries, there are other possibilities. Some people find that a single life is the one for them, but if you pray, you'll get an answer.

Some people say, 'Oh, I've prayed for a husband and now I believe the first person I meet will be the one!' or 'I've prayed for my partner, so I'm not going out with anyone until I meet her.' This is fairly dangerous ground—you wouldn't believe how many people have been 'led' to marry *my husband*!! At times it almost amounts to blackmail, saying 'The Lord's told me to marry you.' So please be very careful!

In some of the other chapters I've talked about giving the Lord your problems and leaving them with Him, and then getting on with the normal run of things. It's the same with this. You pray about it, leave it with the Lord and just go about life knowing that God's working everything out for you. This means if someone asks you out and they are nice and you want to go . . . then fine. Maybe after a few weeks you'll find this isn't

Mr or Mrs Right, and so you cool off.

Now, I know you don't want me to say this . . . but if you've prayed about it, then the Lord is going to find you another Christian. So that non-Christian you've been eyeing up is not in the running! Sorry. It's possible that you know someone in your church who married a bloke who wasn't a Christian, and now he goes to your church and everything's wonderful. Well, it happens, but I wouldn't stake my life on it.

I know many other people who have married non-Christians and the only way they've had any peace in their marriage is for the Christian to stop going to church and stay at home. It's an easy solution for a quiet life—many Christians fall into that trap, and before long they leave their faith altogether. There's a verse in the Bible, 1 Corinthians 7:16, that says you have no way of knowing if you can convert your partner—and it's a very high risk to take.

Perhaps I should add though, that it's more than important that you have non-Christian friends! There's nothing wrong with that and it's good for you—only don't go getting romantically involved with them.

In schools, John and I sing a song called 'Terry don't do it.' It's a very popular song and it's all about a bloke named Terry who's the leader of the Christian Union in his school. He fancies a girl named Tracey who's a year younger than him and very very nice. Unfortunately, Terry's the kind of guy who takes life fairly seriously and Tracey isn't. Tracey looks at life as one big laugh, she doesn't believe in God and the last place she would want to spend her Sundays is in church. Terry, on the other hand, is 100% committed to his life as a Christian and is a regular churchgoer.

The attraction between Terry and Tracey is quite strong and Terry is toying with the idea of asking Tracey out. We wrote the song from the point of view that regardless of how much they liked each other, they had too many opposing views and the relationship wouldn't last. (The whole story can be read in my 'Bad Boy' books.)

Nearly every time we sing this song, it provokes a reaction from school kids—some for and some against. Lots of Muslim teenagers have told us how they feel about being in the same situation with their own faith, and other kids have told us about sad situations with their own parents believing different things. I think that just the fact that a pop song can stir up so many strong feelings in people is a sign that this is a real big problem in a lot of people's lives. It even went to the extent that we had to write another song called 'Tracey', just so that Tracey's feelings were on record too!

We've talked briefly about the sex thing . . . and I don't want to harp on about it, so I'm just going to give you the bits you need to know. OK? We have an enormous number of Christian kids asking us questions like this:

> 'My boyfriend and I live miles from each other, as he is at college and I'm at home. As we only see each other

once a month, surely I owe it to him to sleep with him?'

'My girlfriend and I are engaged. We're planning to get married in four months. What's the difference between sleeping with her now, and four months later? We're going to get married anyway.'

'All my friends are doing it. I'm the only one left with no experiences to talk about!'

There is a common denominator to all of these problems. They are all asking the same question: 'CAN I HAVE SEX BEFORE MARRIAGE?' The short answer of course is 'No'. It doesn't actually matter how you phrase the question . . . the answer is still the same, as if you had wrapped an identical present up in different coloured paper, but when you open it and look inside, it's the same present.

So has God said 'No' just to spoil your fun? Of course not! I know that you can give me at least six reasons why sleeping around is stupid, even if you think it's a rotten rule. And believe me, when God created Adam and Eve and the Garden of Eden, He was into creating love and beauty and nature and happiness. It was the other bloke who was into hate, ugliness and disease. What I'm saying is that God did not invent AIDS as a punishment for people having casual sex—but He did lay down guidelines for how you could avoid it! And disease isn't the only reason of course. One of the saddest results of sleeping with someone outside marriage . . . is heartache. Despair, loneliness and even suicide can be the result.

We met a girl on a Christian holiday and on the last day of the holiday she came to us with her boyfriend. She was fifteen, he was fourteen. She was pregnant. We sat and talked for quite a while, trying to find out whether their parents were liable to disown them or hold out their arms and console them. They were a bit divided, but the girl thought her parents would finally be OK, and the boy thought his parents would probably want his girlfriend to move in with them, so they could help look after the baby. It was all very sad, as neither of them had thought about the consequences and they looked so pathetic and scared, sitting there talking to us.

A few weeks later, I had a phone call from that same girl. She was whispering and she wouldn't leave her number. There was no one else in her house, but she was frightened that someone might come in while she was phoning. She told me that her father was taking her to hospital the next day to have a abortion.

I was shocked and upset, as both she and her parents were Christians. And then she said something that made me realise she had no idea of the enormity of the crisis she was about to go through.

She said: 'Will you pray for me, because I have exams the day after and I'm worried I'll fail them because of being in hospital the day before.'

This young girl was treating an abortion with no more feeling that having a tooth out. She was much more upset about the date clashing with her exams than the fact that she was going to have a living baby pulled from her insides and thrown in a bin.

I never heard from her again, and I had no way of contacting her. I suspect the aftermath of the abortion would have scarred her for ever, and she'll always have that life on her conscience . . . especially as she grows older and marries and has a family.

God didn't say 'No' to spoil your fun. He said it because He loves you and He doesn't want you to have to go through that kind of hell on earth.

Sex was designed to be your wedding present from God. Unopened until the day. An experience designed to bring you and your partner together in a way that's unique. It was designed to keep you together 'Till death you do part'.

'Purity' is not a trendy word.

'AIDS' is.

8

'How come God doesn't speak to me?'

Dear Sue,

I read this book recently about this bloke who heard from God ever such a lot. In fact God seemed to speak to him every day. How come God's never spoken to me? Am I doing something wrong?

I shouldn't think so! God isn't like that. It's more likely that you've never asked Him to lead you! 'Being led' is one of those great Christian mysteries— the thing that happens to everyone else, but no one will tell you how it's done! OK, let's find out what it's all about . . .

What is it?

It's normally a response from God to something you've prayed about. Say, for instance, you have been praying about a friend of yours (let's call him Josh) who has a problem, and you want to help but you don't know how.

Then the next day you see Josh and he says to you, 'I'm in a such a mess, and I really don't know where to turn.'

And before you know it you find yourself saying, 'How about telling your dad?' You're astonished because you know he never talks to his dad and it's a stupid thing to say.

But he turns round on his heels and says 'Hey! That's really strange, I was wondering if I had the nerve to do that!'

Before you know it, Josh and his dad are best mates and all's right with the world . . . OK, that's a lousy example, but that's what it's about. You pray about a situation and ask the Lord to give you a bit of wisdom about it. The next thing you know, you're talking to your friend . . . your throat's gone all dry as you say these words that you know you must say—but at the same time it seems pretty stupid, and wham! it's as if someone turned on the light!

How do I know it was real?
Because of one very important factor . . . Josh had already been toying with the idea himself! You didn't actually tell him anything he didn't already know! But you didn't know that! So if you like, you were working blind here. You said the right thing at the right time, without realising you were almost repeating his thought! Amazing eh? Bear with me on this, as it requires your train of thought. Here's the process we were dealing with . . .

YOU prayed about a situation . . . YOU asked the Lord to help you help Josh . . . At round about the same time, JOSH is praying, 'Lord I don't know what to do.' . . . The Lord impresses on JOSH that he should talk with his father, and JOSH thinks it's a crazy idea . . . then, YOU show up and at the right moment blurt out, 'I think you should talk to your dad!' . . . JOSH is gobsmacked because he's been feeling the same . . . YOU are just as gob-smacked because he tells you that! . . . You've been led! That's how it works on a regular basis.

Of course, we all know people who feel 'led' so often—it makes you feel as if you can't even be living in the same world! But I wonder how often they have actually been right in what they've said or done? Let me tell you of a few instances which I think were decidedly dodgy:

We knew a Christian postman (let's call him Pat!!) who was always feeling led. He was probably one of the worst witnesses to the Christian life we've ever come across. Mainly because he was so busy being led, that he never actually did any work! He would go on his rounds posting letters and handing out tracts at the same time. Every now and then he would feel led to talk to someone for an hour or so on the wonders of being a Christian. Sounds great . . . but unfortunately he was meant to be working. By the time he got back from his first round— everyone else was halfway through their second! Strangely enough he got the sack and a bad reputation for being lazy. Maybe Pat was only trying to be a good Christian . . . or maybe he had read one too many of those books you've been reading!

Another guy I knew used to appear regularly in the record shop I worked at:

'Whatcha Mark!' I would call cheerfully. 'No work today?'

'Na,' he would reply. 'I really didn't think I should go.'

'Why's that then?' I would ask, losing my grin and already guessing the answer.

'Well, it was strange, you know—I got out of bed this morning and I really felt the Lord saying "Go to the record shop." It was a really really strong sensation.' (Well, funnily enough, the Lord hadn't said a word about it to me . . . so I was suspicious.)

'Why do you think that was then, Mark?' I asked.

Mark scratched his uncombed head and replied, 'I don't know, but I'm sure He will show me the reason for being here.'

'Hummphh,' I replied (which roughly translated means 'I don't believe you—what a load of rubbish—push off.')

That whole day was spent with Mark listening to records at my shop. Not a thing happened . . . not a thing. And I wasn't at all surprised. You can't go around using 'I feel led' as an excuse for not feeling like going to work!

It's so easy to use it as an excuse. I remember one time when I was working in a record shop near the Old Bailey. It was a fairly ordinary day until out of the blue there was this strange and extremely frightening noise. It sounded as if God had ripped the sky open with His bare hands—and it frightened us all silly. I

remember running to the door and looking up to
see what had happened and it was all totally calm
again, and then there was this enormous rocking
sensation and we could hear records falling off
their racks in the basement. The girl that I worked
with was quite hysterical by now and I wasn't sure
whether I should be hitting her round the face like
they do in films . . . I decided instead to shake her
shoulders.

If it had happened today, your first thought
would have been 'There's been a bomb blast!' But
as it happened this was the first bomb of many to
start hitting London. Our shop was just around
the corner to the Old Bailey . . . in fact my
husband John had actually walked past the car
being examined by two policemen a few hours
before it exploded into millions of pieces.

At the time we had no idea at all what had
happened, and then the chaos started. There were
firemen with gas masks and huge pickaxes
rushing around everywhere, you could hardly see
the street for blue flashing lights and as we were
by Fleet Street, the reporters were rushing into our
shop and grabbing the phones out of our hands in
an effort to get the story covered. It was an awful
occasion, one in which the caretaker of our
building died . . . and I never went back. Call me a
coward, but it shook me rigid and I had no desire
to see the wreckage again.

What has all this got to do with 'being led'?
Well, my boss—a terrific lady with a loud voice and
an intellect that frightened the *Times* crossword—
was rather upset that I left and insisted to anyone
who asked after me, that I had received 'divine

guidance' to go. She knew very well that I was a Christian and did her best to accommodate the fact by running downstairs every time she wanted a good swear and apologising for anything vaguely 'sinful'. So, although it was very nice of her to insist that God had led me to leave . . . it wasn't actually true! I was just too scared to go back! Gosh, why do I keep baring my soul to you like this?

OK, just one more and then we'll get round to times when 'feeling led' was certainly the right thing. A while ago we had a disastrous flood in our recording studio. Thousands upon thousands of gallons of water poured through a burst mains pipe outside and into our cellar. We were in the middle of having our studio kitted out with all the right bits and pieces (acoustic tiles, pine wood ceilings, funny-shaped bits that make the sound better, etc.) On top of this we also had a fair amount of musical equipment in there at the time. Apart from the 'shock horror', wellington boots, fire brigade and insurance men, we also had about £15,000 of damage. Boy! Did we ever get some prophecies about that!!

Admittedly. most people felt sorry for us and I think some folk even felt led to tell us things in sympathy . . . but we were told everything from 'The Lord will spread a rainbow over the studio and it will prosper,' to 'The Lord is telling you to stop playing this rock music and serve Him in a more useful way.' Don't you just love it!?

Now, whichever way you look at it—they can't all be right, as the views were totally opposed. So somewhere along the line someone either had their lines crossed or they were telling porkies! So we waited until the Lord had a word with us. Happily we were convinced that in the long run things would be even better than they were, as this wasn't the first time the Lord had let something of ours be destroyed only to build something more beautiful in its place. (But that's another story . . .)

So anyway, let's get on to people who got it right, or nearly—and how they felt about it.

We had tea with a couple last year while we were working in some schools in the area. We'd not met them before but we had a nice time with them that evening (probably because they had a dog . . . I like people who like animals . . .) Then just before we left, the lady of the house came to me with an envelope (I started praying like mad that it contained a cheque for a million pounds . . .) and she said, 'I'd like to give you this. The Lord spoke to me about you and John and I wrote down what He said. I'd love you to read it, and if you think it's a load of rubbish just throw it away.' Immediately I wanted to read it, because this woman had the right attitude. She wasn't saying, 'I definitely know this is for you blah blah . . . ' but she was humble enough to admit that she could be wrong. At the same time you already felt that she had it right. 'It probably sounds a bit silly to read, but I felt it very strongly,' she said.

All right, I'll tell you what it said and it *does* sound silly but believe it or not she got it right! It couldn't have made much sense to her. Anyway, in the letter she said she saw John as a fridge (bear with me . . . please!) and it was as if I was the party hostess. I was entertaining people and then I showed them over to the fridge. People were sighing because it was as if they could see through the fridge (kind of X-ray visions . . .) but the door wasn't open, so they couldn't see properly. Then I went over and opened the fridge door and everyone could see the stacks of goodies inside.

Interpretation? . . . Well, that's really how John and I work a lot of the time. We sing some songs and then I spend some time chatting the audience up and making them laugh, and then we maybe sing some more songs and when the time is right, John steps forward and preaches the gospel. So the picture very much verified what we do.

Sometimes, driving home late from a concert or mission, one of us will say to the other; 'That was a good hostess and fridge night wasn't it?' It's nice to know that God sees it the same way.

Now, this particular prophecy was not saying how things were going to be in the future, but it was more like a confirmation that what we were doing at the time was right. A more astonishing time was when we were shopping in Boots in Cardiff with a preacher friend of ours. We were quite happy mooching around when suddenly our friend Johnny stopped and grabbed our arms.

'See that geezer over there?' (Yes, he's a cockney, same as me!)

We nodded, almost praying we were not thinking the same thing.

'God's just told me he's training to be a Mormon priest. He used to be a Baptist, but he's gone wrong,' he muttered.

John and I looked at each other. We knew
Johnny well, and realised that if God had given
him this word of knowledge, then it was almost
bound to be right . . . it's only that we were in the
middle of Boots and we just knew what was going
to happen next! Before we knew it, we were
standing around this man, with Johnny telling
him that God was telling him to come back to Him
straight away, and to give up the Mormon
priesthood. By now, John and I were grinning
nervously at the rest of the shoppers and looking
for the exits.

Would it finish there? Not likely! Before we
knew it, Johnny was praying for this guy. . . . in
Boots! The guy was in floods of tears as he
confessed that everything was true and he prayed
there and then to come back to the Lord.
Stunning! You read about these things . . . but to
be there when it happens is something else!

We've often chatted to Johnny about these
times of 'feeling led' and he says that the Lord had
to teach him gradually when to speak and when
to keep his mouth shut. It took quite a few years
to stop the eagerness overriding the timing. So
even when God does speak to you, there is a time
and place to deliver what He's given you.
Sometimes the time and place *might* be Boots . . .
but it's more likely to be round at someone's house
after tea!

If you feel it's really important for you to be
used in this way, then you must pray a lot about
it. God isn't going to use you if you're not
prepared to sacrifice. The more you are in tune

with the Lord the more He can count on you in difficult situations, but don't expect it to fall into your lap. God wants to use all of us, but it will always come down to how much time we give Him and how much desire we have for God to use us. Whatever.

9

'How do you give God EVERYTHING?'

Dear Sue,

How much do I give God? I know lots of songs that say 'Give Him Your All'—but how much is that in real terms? How do you go about giving someone 'your all'?

I shall take encouragement from the fact that you actually want to know! You think to yourself, 'I'm just some kid at school, I've got a paper round and I'm good at football . . . so what can God possibly get out of that?'

The day I became a Christian, I realised how important it was going to be to really go for it. I don't know what made me feel like that from Day One, but I just thought, 'If God loves me this much, I ought to go for it.' In one way it was great because I hadn't had time to get 'spiritual' about it, I didn't know all the things a Christian 'should' do, so I just went on how I felt. It seemed really important to me to tell my friends about Jesus and it seemed important to go to church and suss out all these new friends I'd suddenly found . . . and then I read this great verse in my very new crispy Bible. It said:

> *I was put to death on the cross with Christ, and I do not live any more—it is Christ who lives in me.*
>
> (Galatians 2:20)

I thought this was a brilliant verse; it was like a brand-new start. My old life was gone and now I had this new one that Jesus was in control of, so as far as I was concerned He was now the boss!

I did a lot of good things and I did a lot of stupid things, all in the name of Jesus, and I'm sure He must have shaken His head in exasperation at me at times (still does . . .) but I was just eager to get on with the job.

I had only been a Christian around eighteen months when I married a minister! (Yes, John's a pastor!) We had a church in the East End of London and I grew up in my Christian life pretty fast as we dealt with all sorts of inner-city problems. Then our lives changed radically when we found ourselves transferred to the wonderful island that is Guernsey. It was on this island that I started learning what giving your all was all about.

We had virtually no young people in our church, and because of this we decided to change a few things. We started up a group to sing on Sunday nights. This wasn't to be a group to lead worship or anything like that—this was a group created to sing the gospel. Sunday nights had always been advertised as the 'Gospel Service', so we thought it was about time we did something positive. Our group 'Dunamis' sang evangelistic words to up-to-date records, and I suppose at the start it was a bit of an eyebrow-raiser with the congregation.

Guernsey is a very small place, and we hadn't been singing that long in our church when we found ourselves in great demand for other churches' services and then youth meetings and so on. In fact life was getting very busy!

Shortly after this, we had our first invitation outside church—we were asked to sing in a hotel. This was swiftly followed by a few nightclubs and an old folks' home! Singing in places that were not church, by any stretch of the imagination, was a lot different. Christians tend to just sit and smile and nod at you, whereas we got the feeling that everyone was listening to the words here, and the words were very evangelistic! It made you terribly conscious of the fact that you were a Christian standing up in front of an audience that largely wasn't! However, the results were amazing—we had people coming over to us in between sessions asking us about our faith and why we did what we did. It just made you think, 'Why don't I do this all the time?'

That thought was probably the start of our 'giving Him everything'. As time went on, we found ourselves playing to more and more places outside church. Clubs, bars, discos—it was quite incredible, and all the time the Lord was saying to us, 'Look! See what you could do if you let me

95

have everything! You could turn the world upside down—all you've got to do is let go of everything you hold dear, and let me take over!'

You see, the thing was, we had got to the position where we had to make a choice. We could see that the Lord could use us greatly in evangelism and He kept giving us verses of Scripture to back it up. There were words from other people also, and then came the opening. We felt almost pushed into a corner and the whole band had been praying 'Lord, we want to do this, we want to be full-time on the road spreading Your Word . . . but how??' The opening, that's how. We received a letter from our church headquarters. It was the kind of circular letter that you get every few months telling you who's moved, who's had a baby, etc., but this time there was a bit on the end that said, 'We are looking for a team of young people willing to tour around Britain for a year. We would like them to encourage youth groups and help with evangelism in areas across the country. If you have any young people in your church who would willingly give up a year of their lives to serve God in this way, please let us know. They must be able to play an instrument, sing or give a testimony. We are also looking for a leader to take charge of the operation.'

It was as if God had written us a letter! Here we were . . . a ready-made team! Look no further! Forget trying to get a team together— we're here!! Leader complete, music, testimonies . . . it couldn't be more right!

We sat and worked out a great speech and then phoned head office to offer ourselves for the job. And you know what it's like when you have the words in front of you and you're totally prepared for it . . . yes, you're right, he was out!

The next day while the members of the band were all at work, and Mutley (our dog) had taken John for a mad dash round the park, the phone rang. It was the bloke from Head Office! I was all alone in the house, the piece of paper with our well-rehearsed speech on had conveniently flown to outer space and my only way out of now carving this up completely was to tell Mr Corsie that John was out.

'Oh well, never mind,' he said. 'You can tell me what it was about.'

Panic! 'Oh, ah, umm, well I think John could tell you an awful lot better . . . ' I stalled frantically.

'Well, can't you just give me an idea?' he asked encouragingly.

So that was it. I had to deliver some garbled message of how we were the people for the mission. We could sing harmonies and give testimonies and John was a perfect leader . . . I made such a mess of it, and at the end of my speech he said, 'Yes.'

Nothing else, just 'Yes.'

I was dumbstruck! In fact I was amazed he'd understood a word I'd said, and then he explained.

'I had been sitting at my desk praying about this team. I felt sure it was right, and yet I'd hardly heard a word from anyone. Then I looked down at my desk and there was a note that just read 'Phone John Ritter'. Well I have, and you've

97

offered me the entire package. God is in this, the
job is yours if you feel you should take it on.
There's no salary, it's only on for a year, I don't
know how you'll do it—but go for it.'

So that was it. That night the five members
of the band sat round and discussed what all this
actually meant, and we came up with a pretty
mean list!

1. We were not officially getting
    paid, therefore we would have to
    rely on gifts from the churches
    we played for.
2. We were all going to leave the
    island of Guernsey. Some of the
    lads had lived there all their
    lives.
3. We didn't have the kind of music
    equipment we needed to do the
    job.
4. We were all going to lose our
    jobs!
5. We didn't have any money.
6. We had nowhere to live in Britain
    when we got there.

Quite an impressive list, eh? But the
solutions to all these problems were twice as
horrific:

1. We would have to pray all our
    money in each week of our lives
    on the road.
2. We were going to leave everyone

we loved and they were never
going to understand,

3.   The only way we were going to
get equipment, was to sell things
we valued to us to buy it.

4&5. Oh all right, we were going to
have to sell everything we owned
to get this ministry off the
ground.

6.   We had to pray for a house!!

How did this work in real terms?? Well, we
all had a good look at the things we owned that
would actually bring in money. Unfortunately
John and I didn't own the church house so we
couldn't sell that, but we could sell our contents
. . . so away went the fridge and the washing
machine, the record player, the armchairs, the
curtains, the carpets—in fact the lot! The fellas in
the band sold their record players, old guitars,
football boots—one guy had a car to sell, it just all
had to go. Funnily enough we made the papers
with this harebrained scheme of ours, but we were
very happy and extremely excited about the whole
thing. Giving up everything you own is a wild and
scary feeling. I'm sure you realise that if God is in
something as crazy as this, He's going to do
everything in His power to make sure it leaves
the ground. So we then found ourselves in the
middle of a wonderful time full of miracles and
disasters.

We had a phone call from a minister in
Rugby, who said he had heard about our calling

and was concerned about where we would live when we came over to England in just a few weeks.

We cheerfully told him that we didn't know, but we were confident that God had it all in hand.

'That's what I thought.' he said. 'Well, our church is trying to sell the church manse and it's still up for sale. I'm going to move into the new house, so we decided that if you needed a house to live in, you could live in the church manse for a year. We'll take it off the market, and it's yours until the year is up. After that, you're on your own.'

We had a house! We had somewhere to live! As fast as we were giving things up, we were gaining new ones, it was incredible!

We then hit the boring bits—people kept coming up to us and saying, 'This is a stupid idea, it will never work!' 'How do you think you're going to stay alive?' 'You are doing the wrong thing. John should stick to being a minister of a church!' 'You will never get enough bookings to survive like that!'

By the time we boarded the boat to come to Britain, we had a house, a van, some music and PA equipment and a year's bookings!

The tale of 'life on the road' is never-ending. We have been doing the same job for fifteen years—although for the last six years it's been just John and myself. God told us to do it, we felt completely sure that it was right and we're still here! We go through good times and bad times and the Lord can trust us a little more these days, but He still has to get us out of a jam now and then.

I think part of proving that you've given God your all is that you see Him working in your life. About six months ago John and I got into a right old mess with our finances—some of it was our fault, but there were also last-minute cancellations that left us strapped for cash. We prayed and prayed about it but didn't seem to get any answer, and we've never told people if we were in trouble, we've always just prayed. But this time it looked as if our ministry was going to fold if we didn't sort out the cash crisis, so we went to some very close friends and borrowed some money. It was awful, but we didn't know what else to do. A few months later, those same friends came to us and said, 'Look, we don't think that God is happy with you being in debt, so we'd like to wipe the slate. Keep the money and stop worrying about what you owe.'

Worry? Us? We'd been terrified! It was such a relief to know our debt was cleared and that the Lord had been in it! Then in the very same month, we received an invoice for something we were buying gradually (it was the only outstanding bill we had.) Across the word INVOICE someone had typed CREDIT. We thought this must have been a mistake because we were talking a lot of money here, so we phoned and queried it (we're terribly honest like that . . .), and were told that the firm involved felt it was time to tithe some money and had decided to strike out our invoice. 'You don't owe us anything,' they said.

We are still dumbfounded as this only happened very recently and we can only thank God that once again He has confirmed that He wants us where we are.

So, looking back, I'd say that God only wants you to give Him your all so He can give you something much better in place of it!

Please don't expect the Lord to treat you the same way He's treated us—that's not what it's all about. You are an individual person and God has a plan for your life, but He can only unfold that plan as you give more of yourself to Him. Now I don't know what He wants of you, but you do. You know in your heart when God's saying 'Do this' and you're saying, 'But God, I don't want to do it that way.' Well, that's your choice.

John always says that when God wants him to do something for Him, all He really has to say is, 'John, do you love me?' If you love God and you've understood what it is to become a Christian, then you'll understand the importance of doing things God's way. It might not be much He wants from you—He's probably not going to ask you to leave home and become a missionary, but He might well ask you to give a testimony or miss out on a football game to do something for Him. Let's face it, if He can't rely on you to miss the football, He's hardly likely to ask you to do something spectacular, is He?

It always comes down to choices. You can be a Christian and toe the middle line, never getting hurt but never doing anything interesting (this is generally referred to as a 'boring Christian life'). Or you can 'Give Him Your All' and watch the most amazing Christian life open out in front of your eyes.

Whatcha gonna do??

10

'Some people get right up my nose!'

Dear Sue,

In a perfect world everything goes right, but in my world it really gets carved up. I try to love everyone and be nice to them—but there are some people who really get up my nose! In all honesty, I could push them through a wall ... what's wrong with me?

It's not you—it's the rest of us!!! Seriously though, I think you're just behaving like a normal human being with emotions and feelings that get hurt and upset and angry at times. Dealing with those feelings is the hard part. It's no good pretending they're not there, so I suppose we'd better get down to talking about them.

My minister (and probably loads before him) always said, 'If you ever find the perfect church—don't join it, you'll only spoil it.' Of course, this perfect church doesn't exist, but the sentiment is a good one. I can well remember when I first became a Christian, going around smiling lovingly at people because I thought that was what you were supposed to do. Now, my family will tell you that to have me floating around the house being nice to people is not natural! Not that I'm not a nice person . . . more that at heart I'm slightly aggressive and enthusiastic in a 'get out of my way' type of way. So all of a sudden to become this airy-fairy person did not fool people for a minute.

I remember going to see an evangelist and being totally overawed by his sense of 'love and peace'. It was very real and he was a great bloke and I thought to myself, 'Yeh! I want to be like that!' And I seriously thought it would be as easy as copying what he did. *And that's where we keep going wrong.* I smiled lovingly at other Christians around me . . . I even smiled lovingly at the evangelist's kids (and they were brats!!) The whole thing was so contagious and I really felt as if I'd made it! I was this Christian who loved everyone, it was really working, life was wonderful! But of course, the minute I got back to good old-fashioned 'Life', it was a disaster. Gritting my teeth, I thought to myself, 'Yes, well, I bet that evangelist has never had to put up with people like my boss! He wouldn't have smiled so nicely if he'd just been given all this typing two minutes before going-home time!'

So what went wrong?

It was the usual thing. I was trying to get one up on God. You know, when you become a Christian, certain things happen. One is that you believe that Jesus died for your sins. The trouble is, most of the time we don't actually believe that

for a fact. If Jesus died to take away our sins . . .
how come I'm still carving it up so badly? We're
not depending on Jesus to do His bit and so we
think we've got to help Him out. If the whole point
of Jesus dying is that I don't have to try any more,
why don't I just let the Lord get on with it?
Goodness knows! But I don't!

When God had this plan of sending Jesus to
die for us, He did it so that we wouldn't have to
worry about doing things wrong and getting
ourselves into a mess any more. God thought to
Himself, 'These people that I've made are having a
hard time trying to keep my commandments—they
really need a way of escape.' OK, so far so good.
Now, Jesus came as our means of escape and He
said to His Father . . . 'I've never done anything
wrong, so I can be the innocent party—lay all of
their blame on me. If you punish me instead of
them, then they won't have to feel bad any more.'
So when we come to Jesus and say, 'I believe you
died for me,' we are getting rid of all those feelings
that make us feel guilty every time we do
something wrong.

Let me tell you about a fella that John and I
met on a trip to Europe a while back. His name
was Nick and he was very much a 'drop out' kind
of bloke. He was probably about nineteen and he
had left a very nice home to seek his own fortune.
He landed up in Holland waiting on tables and
doing odd jobs, until one day someone told him
about Jesus, and his life changed. Happily, he
still looked like a 'drop out', his hair was still all
over the place and he still roamed around the
country. (I just put that bit in, because so many

people seem to think that becoming a Christian has got something to do with changing your appearance . . . Wrong!!) When we met him, he was very excited because in just a few weeks' time, he was going to be baptised in water at a local church. Now, this is a special occasion for anyone, but for Nick it was going to be a real day to remember.

He explained to us that when he became a Christian, he had heard a preacher saying that when you said to Jesus 'I believe you died for me' it was as if you were packing all your sins into a suitcase, taking them to the foot of the cross and saying, 'Here you are Lord, here's my sins of the past, present and future . . . *you* deal with them!' But he went on to tell us that the preacher had then said how sad it was that so many people tend to pick the suitcase up and carry it away with them again. (Just like us when we think we've got to 'try' to love people!)

So Nick had this plan . . . He was going to go to his baptism carrying a suitcase. He was going to walk into the water with his suitcase in his hand and then when he went under the water to be baptised, he was going to let go of the suitcase and come up without it!

'I'm going to show the Lord and all the people at the service, that I mean business with God, and I'm not interested in dragging my past life up ever again!' he said cheerfully.

And that's basically what we need to do! Your future is in God's hands and we need to let God work it out.

How you feel about people is going to depend
on how much of Jesus you've got in your life. If
you let Him into your emotions . . . He'll help out.

I wonder if you smoke—and really wish
you didn't? Perhaps you have a problem with
swearing and find that it's a real hassle and you
can't stop.

On the other hand, maybe you've been really
stupid and overstepped the mark with your
boyfriend or girlfriend.

Maybe you've had a blazing row with
someone you can't do without and you've said
these words . . . 'I'm *never* going to talk to him
again!'

It could be that you can't stop nicking things
. . . nothing major, just little things . . . but it's
getting out of hand.

Well, whatever it is—I can tell you this—you
are going to have one heck of a time trying to cope
with it on your own. Oh sure, you've prayed about
it . . . but then you've done the 'suitcase' thing,
haven't you? You've picked it up and started
again! Well, that's not what Christianity is about.

Listen, you take your hang-up to the Lord
and you say, 'Here You are Jesus, You died for
this, it's Your problem now, not mine.' And you
stop worrying about it. Now, if you seriously do
this, I can guarantee that the Lord will deal with
whatever it is you're worried about.

I'll take one 'for instance', OK?

You smoke. You don't want to smoke—but
you smoke. So you pray about it and then you go
out and buy some anti-smoking tablets, which

taste foul and anyway you carry on smoking. Well, how do you want to stop? Do you want to take the tablets or do you want the Lord to snuff it out for you? It's no good asking the Lord to deal with your problem and then seeking alternative ways of curing yourself. You've either got to let the Lord do this or not. And I'm talking about sin here . . . not healing or general answers to prayer . . . I'm not talking about you praying about passing your exams and then sitting back and letting the Lord give you a pass mark . . . . *I'm talking about you doing something wrong and wanting God to deal with it.*

Jesus either died for ALL your sins or He didn't die for any of them . . . Here's a great verse from the Bible that I think you should keep close by you for times like this . . .

> *If the law could make us right with God,*
> *then Christ's death would be useless.*
> (Galatians 2:21)

We know, don't we, that we can't keep the ten commandments. We can't even keep our temper at times, so if we were under pressure to keep the commandments, we would very quickly lose our salvation. But we live by grace (that is, we believe that Jesus set us free from a guilty conscience). So we can be forgiven for the things we carve up.

But we'd rather not carve them up in the first place. John and I find that because of the nature of our ministry, we get a lot of people demanding our time and attention, and it's not demanding our time and attention, and it's not always convenient. At times like that we really have to try and sort out who needs us the most. (Ooh, that sounds a bit big-headed, doesn't it?) The thing is, a lot of the time the people you really want to be with and the people who need to be with you, are not the same ones!

You know what it's like when you are just about to go out with all your friends on a Saturday afternoon. You get dressed up and the idea is basically to eye up the local talent . . . then just as you're going out of the door, your mum yells out 'Just a minute!' . . . and you know what she's going to say. There she is standing with your little sister. It's agony! And before you can protest she says, 'Take her with you for an hour, she's got no one to play with.' There are no words to describe how frustrating that is! It must happen to every teenager in the universe—but at that moment in time it's you, and you have the choice of staying in and playing with your terrific little sister by yourself or being the pain of the week to your friends by dragging her round town with you.

Now, I know this is not the greatest example in the world—but the thing is, at that time your sister did actually need you more than your friends!

John and I often get faced with similar situations like: shall we go to this live rock concert we've got tickets for? Or shall we go and spend the evening listening to someone pouring out their problems and telling us how everybody hates them? . . . On the other hand there are times when we've actually got an evening in and we've been

109

and hired the video, bought the chocolates and have settled down in front of the telly and the phone rings.

'Oh great!' says someone we don't know. 'I'm so glad you're in . . . that means you are free to come and do a concert for us! We've been let down by this band and the audience will be arriving in two hours!!'

Now, we've never met this Christian organiser, but we already have a vague dislike of him for mucking up our evening off! It's going to be hard to rush upstairs, get dressed for a concert, throw the equipment in the car and dash to some little village in the middle of nowhere to play to three and a half people and a cat (if we're lucky . . .) So most of the time you have to try and put yourself in their shoes . . . The little sister may genuinely feel 'left out' and need a bit of extra attention now and then. And let's face it, if you made time for her on other occasions, she might not feel so lonely when you go without her! The person with problems might be in genuine need of help, and the harassed organiser was probably at his wits' end trying to work out what to do . . . and in all these cases the 'odd one out' is made to feel wanted and extremely happy.

As we talked about earlier in the 'prayer' chapter . . . you also must find time to tell the Lord about the situation—confessing that you haven't got time for this bozo who keeps hanging around wanting attention, and asking the Lord what to do about the situation . . . unfortunately, He is liable to say, 'Well, I had time for you didn't I?'—but there you go!

I suppose the other half of the story is that when you have had a blazing row with someone, or you've hurt someone's feelings, somewhere along the line you've got to say that five-lettered word, 'SORRY'. Yuk! Isn't that the difficult one? I think that a lot of the time, becoming a Christian is a gateway to an awful lot of other things that happen in your life. You know, making the decision to become a Christian is the most important decision of your life, but once you've done that, it really helps you in making other decisions that are still very important. Like where you're going to work, who you're going to marry, how you're going to live. All of these important decisions can now be made with the help of Jesus, and that means making the right decision! Becoming a Christian took a step of faith, and now when you take other steps into unknown territories you take the step with Jesus by your side . . . You know what I'm going to say next don't you??

When you became a Christian, you said an enormous 'sorry' to Jesus for the wrong things you did against Him. So now, every time you have to say 'sorry' you can say it with the Lord's help.

You see? The *big* decision has been made, the *big* step has been taken and the *big* Sorry has been said.

So now we only have to deal with the smaller ones.

'Love is never having to say you're sorry.' I don't think so! Love is *being able* to say you're sorry!

In Ephesians there's that great verse that says, 'Be sure to stop being angry before the end of the day' (Eph. 4:26). You've probably heard people sing about that (an older version is 'Don't let the sun go down on your anger'), and it's a very wise saying. If you can hold on to that verse, it makes saying 'sorry' even easier.

When I first found that verse in my Bible, I had been angry with a friend of mine. He had been trying to tell me that God had told him not to go to work and he felt led to laze about all day. I really tore him off a strip and sent him home with a flea in his ear. Righteous anger?? Not really, I think I was just annoyed with him for being so stupid. But as the day wore on, I remembered this verse, and I was feeling a little bit guilty for giving him such a hard time. He had looked like a dog with his tail between his legs by the time he went home. It was a strange thing, because in a way he was wrong and I was right—and yet I still felt that I had done the most damage. He was a new Christian and I hadn't treated him very well. There must have been other ways to explain to him that he'd got it wrong!

So after work I went round to his house and apologised and showed him the verse in Ephesians.

Funnily enough, at the time I hadn't reasoned out *why* I wasn't supposed to let the sun go down on my anger . . . I just did it because I had seen the verse in the Bible and taken it to be good advice. But of course, the more I thought about it, the more I realised how much we brood on things, and let them go on for days and days— sometimes months and years! Obviously, the longer you harbour a grudge against someone, the worse you are going to feel and the harder it is to say 'sorry'. But when I looked back into the Bible's reasons they were even more serious than mine. If we include verse 27, the whole quote is, 'When you are angry, do not sin, and be sure to stop being angry before the end of the day. Do not give the devil a way to defeat you.'

Ah! I hadn't thought about that. I was just thinking 'in the natural' about how it makes you feel to hold on to anger . . . but the Bible pointed out that the devil will use that time when you were angry and multiply it out of all proportion! And we've all had times when *that's* happened, haven't we? So many lives get ruined by the absence of the word 'sorry'. If we had said 'sorry' ten seconds after we'd carved it up, then the incident would hardly have been noticed, as it is we brood and mull it over and say things that make it ten times worse, then we bring in other people and we're all shouting at each other . . . stupid, isn't it?

We will get it wrong at times and we will hurt other people, but we have the Lord and we have a great handbook in the Bible, so we should be able to sort ourselves out.

Please consult both next time someone gets up your nose!

11

'Why do dads always have to dance in front of your friends?'

Dear Sue,

My visits to church have been spoilt lately by my best friend's dad. He's a great bloke but recently he's taken to 'skipping' around the church every time someone mentions the word 'worship' . . . I can't believe it's for real—I mean not all the time, surely?

Have you ever known a parent *not* to embarrass you?? Seriously, though, I do know how you feel, but dancing is a natural expression (unfortunately at times . . .) and when we experience something that makes us feel great—we dance! Okay, let's get it into perspective . . . How many times have you watched a little kid open his Christmas presents and then all of a sudden he gets to the 'big one'—the one he's been waiting for. He rips off the paper, holds the world's most brilliant Christmas gift in the air and promptly dances round the room with it! He does, doesn't he? When you and your friends are playing some stupid game and you win, what do you do? You throw your arms up in the air and yell 'Yes!!' If you get a ticket to Wembley Arena to see the most spectacular rock band on earth, and your school friends don't get theirs . . . you waltz around the room, waving the ticket at them and singing, 'I'm going to see them, I'm going to see them!!'

You can't have missed the dances that footballers do when they score a goal in the European or World Cup qualifying games. I don't mean the hugs and kisses . . . but the dance in front of the fans. It's celebration time!

So that sorts out the first thing. Dancing is a natural expression of excitement. However, there is an extreme to everything and there are times when it is just a performance. In church a dance can be interpreted as 'Look how spiritual I am'. People do it because it's visual. In other words, it's a display that other people look at. The same as wearing your 'Sunday best' or praying long, loud prayers in the middle of the service. People can sit back and watch and judge for themselves and think 'Gosh! He's so spiritual!' The thing is, we can't see what is going on in that person's mind and heart. It could be that he is harbouring some terrible grudge against someone—but we can't see it. He could have been rotten to his wife before he came out—but we were not there. He might not even believe in Jesus! . . . we are not to know that.

The chances are of course, that he is totally genuine and really enjoying loving the Lord.

Jesus had a lot to say about people who were 'religious' and did all the right things for people to see. He called them 'whitewashed graves' . . . in other words, they looked clean and freshly painted on the outside, but inside there was only death and decay. So we have to be really careful how we act, and why we do what we do.

Why does your friend's dad skip round the church? It's a big question and there are many explanations. At the moment things in the church seem to go in trends. At one time, you couldn't be considered a 'real' Christian unless you clapped your hands to every song. Then if you'd really got it together you would have a go at raising your hands too! After this came the 'new language' and I'm not talking about being baptised in the Spirit . . . I'm talking about saying words like 'radical' 'strategy', 'knowing your heart', 'envisioning' and 'warrior'. You could no longer say 'Hey! that's new!' or 'Got any plans?' or 'You know what I mean?' or 'I've got a good idea' or 'It's tough praying sometimes, isn't it?' *And then* someone said, 'You can't be a real Christian unless you dance!'

I don't know how people get taken in by things so easily, but most of the things in the Christian life should be a natural reaction to being close to the Lord, and not because someone with a bit of a name proclaims the next 'trend'. When it first became popular to dance in church, it came along with hugging and kissing each other 'in the Lord' and seeing which church could have the longest service.

I can remember once, after working hard in a school all week, inviting loads of kids to a church where we were going to give a concert. We were delighted when a lot of the congregation turned up to support us as well as a whole crowd of 13- to 16-year-olds. We had a great time in the concert, and at the end we explained to the kids what it was to be a Christian and how they could get to know God. About thirty teenagers responded to that. Obviously, at this stage we just want to say, 'OK, those of you who want to know more, come and see us now and we will pray and talk with you. The rest of you—thanks for coming, it's been a great night. Cheers!'

As I said, *that's* what we would have liked to do! However, the Christians in the concert decided that you really couldn't have something in the church that didn't involve some praise and worship, so before we could stop them, a couple of blokes came up on to the stage and started leading us all in some chorus or other. Terrific! Here we were with around 150 teenagers who had never been to church in their lives, who didn't know the Lord and had no idea what was going on . . . being thrust into the routine of 'Let's sing "Majesty"! We don't need the words, we all know it!' Our temperature was rising and suddenly shot up as these leaders proceeded to dance all over our music equipment! Microphones were stamped on, keyboards were rocking dangerously, drums were knocked over and they skipped and danced around the stage looking complete fairies.

As a group, we sat with our heads in our hands and didn't dare look up. Most of the kids started to leave, some just out of disinterest, and some scared of what was happening next having been warned about people of the same sex who hug each other!

It was such a disaster. The fact that teenagers had just made decisions for Christ seemed to go completely over their heads in their eagerness to put on the Christian Spectacular, so that everyone could see how much they loved each other.

This unfortunate incident made me very wary of anything 'trendy' in the church. But yes! There is a good side to worship—of course there is—and I'd like to go on now to some of that.

We know a bloke who used to be a real fan of heavy metal music (I mean, he still is . . .) and the highlight of his week used to be to go to the Heavy Metal Club in his home town. Roger became a Christian. He still continued to go to the club, but now he went intent on telling someone about Jesus. 'I just worked on one mate at a time,' he told us. The Lord used him time and time again to bring his friends to Christ and before he knew it there were a whole bunch of them.

The problem now was that they needed a church to accept them as they were and cater for their needs. In this situation they thought it easier to start again. And so they started to meet once a week in the same place as the Heavy Metal Club . . . and it very soon became their 'church'. It grew and grew and they knew they needed help and guidance from other Christians and so they joined themselves to a group of churches that were already happening. *Now* . . . if you would like to experience 'dancing' because you're excited about Jesus . . . this is the place to go. If you have every wondered what David looked like when he 'danced before the Lord' . . . then I think this place would give you a pretty accurate description! In a way, it almost looks like tribal war dancing—you know, all fists in the air and blokes in leather jackets really giving it some welly! There is nothing soppy about it, and nothing 'put on' either.

John and I were privileged to go to Roger's wedding at the same church. My favourite memory of the service is still seeing a massive crowd of people dancing their feet off and somewhere in the middle of it was a girl's hand holding a bouquet high in the air! If you're going to celebrate—you might as well do it properly!

The other thing we sometimes get confused about is that leading worship is a *ministry*, just like evangelising, teaching, pastoring and everything else! It's not something you can learn to do overnight. We are often asked to take part in the Sunday service at the end of the week, and that's fine. John will preach, I will give a testimony or something and maybe we'll sing a few songs. But nine times out of ten we will be asked if we can lead some worship . . . and quite frankly — No! We can't! It's not part of our ministry and there are people far better 'qualified' than us in their own church! Oh sure, we could probably knock up a few choruses . . . but we really don't *lead* worship at all! I think it's great that God is getting together a fantastic band of worship leaders. Graham Kendrick, Rob Newey, Noel Richards, Dave Bilborough and gang are doing an absolutely tremendous job. We are seeing real hymn-writers being born in our time—it's fantastic! And off the back of that, people in churches everywhere are being inspired to worship in new ways. Brilliant!

So now we have a ministry in leading that worship. It's just so helpful having someone at the front of the church ready to guide you through a time of worship. In days gone by, we often just had some bloke saying 'Number 53' and then standing back while the rest of us got on with singing it. A lot of the time, the person at the front didn't even join in the singing, and if he did, he was so far back from the microphone that you couldn't hear him anyway.

A good worship leader will take time to listen to what God has to say and start leading the worship according to that. He will also have the right way of stopping things getting out of hand. The fella who's making a fool of himself leaping around by himself can be calmed down and veered in a different direction by someone leading worship. I've seen many a minister during a prayer time very tactfully shut up a long-winded prayer or an hysterical 'vision'. It's the same thing with worship.

If you have a good worship leader in your church, it might be a good idea to have a word with him. See how he or she feels about dancing and various types of free expression. It could be that they've been waiting to hear from other people before sorting it out. On the other hand of course, they may feel this guy is 'in the Spirit' and doing the right thing. It's worth having a talk though.

There are many ways to worship Jesus and you shouldn't be bound by only experiencing one way.

The bottom line of this problem, however, is as I said in the beginning . . . adults are a constant embarrassment to kids. There was a wonderful sketch on TV a while ago with a teenager and his friend watching *Top of the Pops*. In comes his dad who immediately starts bouncing round the room clicking his fingers and exclaiming 'Hey! What's this? It's got a good beat!!' The kids of course just shrivel up in a corner and pray to die! Adults always have the idea that you would really like them to join in with your fashion and style—and that's where the bopping in church has become a problem.

Hand-clapping and dancing became trendy a while back and now the people who started it off are in their thirties and married with kids. Unfortunately, they think it's *still* trendy to do this and can't for the life of them understand why *you* don't want to do it! Hence the shouts of 'Come on Matt!' and looks of 'Gosh! Just look what you're missing!' every time a chorus is played. I wish I had the answer to this problem . . . I guess we can only pray that the next trend will include 'Visual Aid Commitment'—where we all just sit down and watch the video. (But your dad will still want to wear the T-shirt!!)

12

'I'm new in my school . . .'

Dear Sue,

I've just moved to a new area and joined a new school. Last week I went to the Christian Union for the first time—it was the pits! At my last school, there were fifty of us but this school has only six and they are so boring. What do I do now?

So, all your worst crises have come to a head at the same time, haven't they! It's bad enough having to leave your friends behind at your old school, without having to try and find a whole load of new ones at the new place.

You don't say how long you've been at your new school, but you do sound as if you're trying very hard to make it just like home! Unfortunately, you have to realise that you have moved on and things will be different. You are in a situation where you really need to count to ten before you do anything. People won't appreciate it if you try to muscle in and change everything! So, things have to happen slowly.

I well remember being in a situation in church, where all we young people went to a brilliant Christian holiday event. It was the first time we'd been on anything like it and we were struck dumb by the amount of hand-waving and clapping and dancing around that was happening there. Of course, we wanted to try this out, and we spent the whole week leaping around and praising the Lord as if it was going out of fashion! We learnt ten million new choruses and were bursting to get back to our church and let rip . . . which, unfortunately for them, was exactly what we did do! We charged into church on Sunday morning and sat in the front row and the minute the first note hit the piano we leapt to our feet, swaying from side to side, and sang ourselves silly!

You see, in our minds, if the rest of the church saw us doing these things—then it was obvious, we thought, that they would automatically think 'Wow! This is terrific!' and leap up to join us . . .

HOWEVER! Quite a few things did happen and none of them were the results we were expecting. For a kick-off, the remainder of our young people, who didn't go to the holiday event, felt completely resentful. They sank further back in their seats and folded their arms and sulked for all they were worth! The people directly behind us were furious, because they couldn't see a thing in front of them for our mindless arm-waving. The older people in the church thought we'd been somewhere totally satanic and the ones that didn't march out stayed and prayed for us! The trouble was, I don't think *one person* enjoyed our display.

Later on, when we sat down and discussed the situation properly, it occurred to us that maybe we had been a bit too hasty, a bit too enthusiastic and about a thousand tons too insensitive. To our church it was as if we were waving a ten-foot banner proclaiming 'WE'VE GOT SOMETHING YOU HAVEN'T, NYAH NYAH! IT'S A SECRET AND WE'RE NOT GOING TO TELL YOU ABOUT IT . . .WE'RE JUST GOING TO SHOVE IT IN YOUR FACES!!!' Oh all right then, a twenty-foot banner!

The thing was, because of our stupid behaviour, it took us ages to get the church to even think about praising the Lord in a different way, let alone getting them to join in! We had to start by making friends with them all over again, and getting their trust back. When we finally made it back to civilisation again, a few of the congregation did come up to us and say, 'Actually, it was rather nice to see the young people in the church doing something for a change. We've never seen them sit in the front row before, they're always at the back. We didn't really want to dampen their enthusiasm, but we wished they had gone a little slower for our sakes.'

The point of this story I hope is a bit obvious. You have just walked into a Christian Union that's dying on it's feet—and if you're not careful, you're going to find yourself in the same situation as we were!

Your Christian Union will not appreciate it if you go there and every other sentence begins,

'Well, in *our* Christian Union we used to . . . '. As much as you might want to be helpful, you've got to play it cool.

I have no doubt that if the CU is as bad as you say it is, then the chances are they will welcome you with great enthusiasm and look to you for new ideas. . . but take it slowly.

Right, that's my first point out of the way . . .TAKE IT SLOWLY!

Second point—please don't give up on it! The reason a lot of CUs are having a hard time is because the only people who could help them won't touch them with a barge pole! Now, this is not helpful! I know it's difficult to let yourself be associated with a bunch of dull people . . . but they really do need you! I think one of the hardest things about school Christian Unions is that they change every year. This is bound to happen depending on who runs it and where the ideas are coming from. A lot of the time, it flows from a handful of sixth-formers who really get in there and make it happen—and then they leave! Agghh!

We were playing in a school very recently where this very thing was happening. The Christians in the sixth form were magnificent! Their enthusiasm knew no bounds and the rest of the school (Christians or not) thought they were wonderful too! Trouble was, this was their last term and everyone was going to miss them terribly. However, in this particular situation, the sixth-formers had already got a 'cunning plan'. They had spent most of their last two terms training up the fifth-form Christians ready to take over! Now, that was a marvellous thing to do . . . we don't always like handing things over to someone else, but in this case they did the right thing.

A Christian teacher can make or break a CU as well. Sometimes it works really well to have a teacher in charge, if that teacher is popular at school (enough said, I think . . .).

Anyway, now let's get back to you. I hope some of the things I've said will make sense, if not already, then in a while. It will be a worthwhile thing for you to sit back and listen for a few weeks while you find out exactly why the CU is such a disaster area. Have *they* just lost a load of older members? Maybe there's no one to lead it and they need the help of a teacher but are afraid to ask? Has there been a split of personalities that's caused another half a dozen kids to leave? Are they truly the only Christians in the school?? How long has the CU been operating?

When you've gathered enough facts together, you may start to be in a position to help. It could be that they have just run right out of steam and ideas and need a fresh start. This is where you come in . . . gradually . . . not like we did at our church! If the CU has only six members, then they are very vulnerable and liable to get on the defensive fairly quickly if you criticise them. Right now they need building up and encouraging. (Don't we all!!?) You have a great opportunity for the Lord to really use you here, so it's important to take it slowly.

Right! I suppose you're now wondering how you are going to be seen associating with the CU *and* keep some kind of credibility with the rest of the school, huh?

I know quite a few people who are incredibly good at paying attention to unlovely folk. One guy I know is great for sitting down with someone no one else wants to talk to and really is interested in what the guy's got to say and everything! Naturally enough, the boring bloke all of a sudden starts to bloom as he gets some attention (sometimes for the first time in his life . . . !).

Now, I've often said to Steve, 'I don't know how you do that! He's such a boring bloke and yet you spend all that time with him . . . I'd run out of things to say after two minutes!'

The thing is, although I'm saying, 'Oh yuck, how can you stand to be seen with that fellow?'— what my voice is saying is, 'I admire you!'

And like it or not, your friends will admire you for associating with people they can't put up with. They'll say the same as everyone else . . . he's boring . . . he's not worth bothering with . . . he's not your type . . . but the underlying thing will be admiration for what you're doing, IF you are doing it for the right reason. And the follow-on from that will gradually be, 'Well, if she thinks he's OK to talk to . . . maybe he's not so bad . . . '

So I'm afraid the bottom line is that you have to associate with your CU regardless of who they are or what they're like, because even if you don't, as soon as your friends know you're a Christian, they are going to lump you in the same mould anyway!

So what can you do to help? As I said earlier, any help from you has to come slowly so that the rest of the CU don't see it as a take-over bid. But get in there with suggestions. When they decide they are going to do a discussion on AIDS/ABORTION or whatever, suggest that they get in some Christians who are experts on the subject. Ask them to check around their own churches and see if they have any Christian nurses, doctors, social workers, or anyone else professionally dealing with the subjects in hand.

Doing something like this gets everyone involved. Everyone in the CU can do some checking around their Christian friends and youth groups etc., and come back the following week with the results of their research. You might find that between you, you have a whole panel (three or four) of experts who could spare you an hour or even just half an hour of their time to come to your school and debate the issue.

Once you have a panel you can start an advertising campaign. Make it provocative. Maybe take a couple of weeks to lead up to it by putting up posters with half the information on it. Say, a poster with just the words 'DOES AIDS SCARE YOU?' in big letters and then in much smaller letters at the bottom 'Watch for more details' and then maybe the name of your CU after it. (Yes, we'll get round to talking about names later . . .) Then the next week more posters with 'AIDS?? TALK TO THE EXPERTS!', then in smaller letters 'next Friday' plus information of the room, time, etc. Then on the actual week 'AIDS . . . IS IT GOD'S PUNISHMENT? WHAT DO YOU THINK?' and in small letters 'Put your point across to the experts . . . Dr R. Smith, Nurses Wood and Jones, and Mr D. Roland, psychiatrist'. And again the time and place, but this time in bigger letters.

This kind of thing will guarantee you a non-Christian audience and give you a platform for putting across a Christian viewpoint on a serious matter. Don't use it to try and preach to everyone, but just to introduce yourselves to the rest of the school, to show them that you're concerned for them. Once you start doing this kind of event every now and again, you will start to earn a bit of respect.

The nice thing is, that everyone in the CU can be involved—whatever their skills are. You need people to organise the official invitation of the experts to your school. You need someone brave enough to go the the Head and let him know of your plans and get his approval (This is a worthwhile plan—although you may not need his go-ahead, it would be great to let him see you using your free time in a valuable way!) Then of course, someone has to draw the posters and a couple of you need to pin them up in appropriate places. (If you are allowed, the loo is an excellent place . . . well, I mean, everyone has to go there, don't they?) So already you have used most of your CU members.

A quick word about names before we go on to more ideas. To give your CU a name is about the most important thing! Having gone to loads and loads of them all over Britain, we came to the conclusion that the ones with good names seem to get more respect from the rest of the school.

We often visit a CU more commonly known as SCUM. This might not sound like such a good idea to you—but it's worked wonders in their school. When we came to play in assembly, loads of kids came up to us and said, 'Is this to do with SCUM? They get all the good ideas!' SCUM, by the way, stands for School Christian Union Meeting. Over a few years they have come to be greatly admired by everyone for their antics and outlandish events . . . and everyone thinks they're great! And what's more . . . everyone knows that they are a Christian organisation!

Another good name we came across was CRASH which stood for 'Christians Running Around Singing Hallelujah!' Wonderful, isn't it?? There's also YOYO (You're Only Young Once) . . . and NAM (Not Another Meeting!) and CRUNCH, but I can't remember what it stood for! Anyway, they are just a few ideas, and I'm sure you can come up with one equally as good for yours. It's just so much easier to have a poster that ends

C. R. A. S. H. Room 25. 12.30.

than

Christian Union. Science Lab. 12.30.

Don't you agree?

So, once you've got the ball rolling, I'm sure you will find that you're not the only 'normal' member of your CU. Hopefully some of your ideas will help other members to exert themselves and, best of all, bring new people into the group.

More ideas? . . . Well, keep going with the debates every now and then. Try 'War and Peace'

131

with Christian members of the armed forces, 'Law and Order' with local Christian policeman, etc., and if you're brave enough you could even do one on 'Teachers and Pupils' with any Christian teachers, giving an insight into the problems teachers face and various way of dealing with right and wrong. If you think you can hold it together then maybe it won't hurt to get some Christian soldiers and a few pacifists together. Or some Christian politicians and some non-Christian politicians talking about 'Ethics and Morals' or 'Keeping Sunday Sacred'.

Then, for a 'special' you could maybe invite some well-known outsiders to come in. Try contacting Christians in Sport . . . again it maybe that you know someone who knows someone who has a famous Christian in their church who would come and speak if they don't live that far away. People like John and I as 'Keep In Step' will come to a school and stay around for a whole week taking RE lessons, music lessons, English lessons, assemblies and lunch-time concerts.

To put on a week-long mission is obviously going to be hard work and you need to get one or two churches to help with this. The churches can provide accommodation, money, follow-up and spiritual backing for you. A schools mission can give your CU a great boost, because once the kids in your school have taken to the group, then the CU become very popular people indeed!

And don't stop there . . . charities and charity events are very popular and there are plenty of Christian charities you can support. So why not think up some great ideas for sponsoring? You can easily get a whole school involved if you come up with things people want to do.

We were at a school recently, where the only people who were allowed to organise something for 'Red Nose Day' were, the Christian Union! Actually that's a great shame for the cause—but the school felt that the CU were the only people who could really organise events, and so they were asked to run it. It couldn't have been better for them! And then there's Easter, Harvest Festivals, general assemblies, leaving parties, Christmas parties! Why should everything you do have to have a Christian emphasis? It's good for you to be seen helping anyway . . . so why not organise the school Christmas party? Make it a lot of fun complete with disco, flashing lights, games and food. Maybe you could subtly have a few posters or banners around—some with the usual Christmas messages on, 'Merry Christmas', 'Have A Great Time' etc., and then maybe a few with things like 'Jesus is for life . . . not just for Christmas' and 'Whose birthday is it anyway??'

Just go for it! I've given you a few ideas here and it would be wise to try them out little by little. You don't want to wear out every idea within a term! So take your time, get to know the CU members and gradually make headway with some of the ideas I've mentioned. I know in the beginning it's going to be difficult for you, but I'm sure you'll never be appreciated as much as you will by supporting your group . . . and usually that starts other Christians coming out of the

woodwork and joining you. If you can, talk over
these things with your youth leader, or your pastor
or maybe even your parents. If they see that you
are keen and seriously want to do something, I'm
sure they will be encouraged to give you a hand.
But above all don't give up!

13

'I think I'm going off Christianity...'

Dear Sue,

This may sound stupid, but I'm frightened of 'backsliding'. I mean, I haven't— but I think I might. Every time I do something wrong, I think 'This is it!'... I've heard some terrible stories of people who turn their back on God and now I can't stop thinking about it!

I've written a few books in the 'Bad Boy At School' series and the most popular request from readers is that I let Bobby Harris (the Bad Boy) backslide! Y'know, everyone wants him to backslide an awful lot more than they want him to actually do something right!

In case you're unsure . . . 'backsliding' basically means 'letting go' or 'losing interest' in Christianity. So it's not so much a case of 'sinning' and causing major carve-ups, as it is just wandering slightly off the path and not being able to find your way back again. In other chapters we've discussed feeling guilty about not

135

praying enough, or not reading your Bible enough—sometimes we use these situations to scare ourselves into thinking we're backsliding. It seems to me that there is much more confusion and worry to teenagers about backsliding than just about anything else!

Why is that? Maybe it's because when we first become Christians, in an effort to get us to every meeting people tell us about the 'horrors' of backsliding. Sometimes it's used as a sort of 'veiled threat' . . . it's a gloomy word hung over our heads like some kind of electric shock treatment. Miss a Bible study and ZAP!! the 'Backsliding Electro Machine' gets you!'

John and I were playing in a school recently where a group of very strong, highly religious Christian kids went. Their parents were part of a Christian movement that banishes an awful lot of 'modern' things. For instance, the kids were not allowed to take computer studies because of the evils of 'modern technology'. They had to sit apart from the rest of the school at lunch time, because they were not allowed to eat with people who didn't say 'grace' or take communion. In fact the craziest thing was that they were also not allowed to stay for the assembly that John and I took, because although we were telling kids about our Christian faith, we were using synthesisers and electric guitars!!

The point I'm coming to is that, at the end of this line was a place where, if they stepped out of the will of their families—*they were disowned*!! If any of the kids were to take an interest in a non-Christian boyfriend/girlfriend, or maybe start to use these modern-day methods, then the effect of what the parents called 'backsliding' would be enough for them to say 'You are no longer my son/daughter.'

I also heard recently of an extreme sect who go to the length of having a 'funeral service' for members of the family who 'stray' or 'backslide'. So as far as they are concerned—if you backslide you might as well be dead! No wonder it tears us up so much! And of course the more people say to you 'You must not do that'—the more tempting it is to give it a try!

I think that in most of the churches I've been in, backsliding is talked of in very hushed tones. It's almost got a sort of gossipy ring to it.

'You know Mrs Landlady? Well, poor thing, I just heard that her husband's started to backslide . . . '

'Oh no! How terrible! How long has it been going on? What is she going to do!?'

Poor old Mrs Landlady—you'd think it was *her* problem, not his! But you see, it has this kind of stigma attached to it. If you've robbed a bank or slept with a whole football team there's hope for you . . . but if you backslide . . . ooh . . . well, tut tut, you might as well keep on sliding.

Stupid, isn't it? For the first two years at the church we now go to, there were people there who always gave us the strangest look whenever we arrived at church. At first I thought it was probably the leather jackets or the purple hair, but I gradually found out it was because we didn't attend our church every week! You see, John and I visit around thirty towns a year, going into seventy to eighty schools, presenting the gospel in music and chat—and of course, if you are travelling all over Britain and Europe as your job, it's highly unlikely that you will attend your home church more than once every five or six weeks. So, we would turn up one Sunday and have conversations like this . . .

Them Hello strangers! How are you?

Us Fine. A bit tired, but fine.

Them (*wary look*) We haven't seen you for a little while.

Us No, we've been to Wigan, Reading, Devon and Southend on schools missions.

Them (*extremely wary*) . . . Oh yes, well. Perhaps we'll see more of you now then.

Us (*patiently*) Not really, we're off again on Wednesday and we won't be back for another three weeks.

Them ('*You-can't-fob-me-off-with-that*' *look*) Well, perhaps you could join us for Spring Harvest. I'm sure the young people would enjoy having you there.

Us (*patience wearing thin*) We will already be there, we're working there.

Them (*put out*) Oh? What week?

Us (*gritting teeth*) All of 'em! We will be leading the youth work!

Them (*totally missing it*) Oh well, perhaps you'll visit us again soon.

The last sentence, by the way, can be interpreted as 'Ah, never mind, we will pray that the Lordwill stop your backsliding and send you back to us.'

After we had been going to our church for several years, we asked the minister if we could become members. He looked slightly taken aback and said he'd come and visit us. When he finally came to our house, and we had a chance to explain our ministry to him, he had a good chuckle to himself. When we asked him what was so funny, he replied, 'I'm awfully sorry, but I had no idea that you came solely to our church! I thought that when you didn't appear for some weeks, you had either gone to another church, or perhaps nowhere!'

I must admit it did have its funny side, but at the same time it was sad that nobody had really bothered to find out. We had been faithful to the same church for two years without anyone realising it! And quite a few people obviously thought we were 'occasional backsliders'. Bloomin' cheek!

But it is so easy to get hold of the wrong end of the stick, isn't it? Absent from church equals backsliding in a lot of people's minds.

I don't actually think people backslide quite that lightly. Backsliding is not the occasional skive from the youth meeting, or the staying in to do homework when you should be at the praise meeting! That's just being busy most of the time.

As I said . . . backsliding is letting go. When you have a major problem in your life, it can cause you to let go of Jesus for a while. I suppose nearly all of us know someone fairly close who has died. In this day and age it has become frighteningly common to have had the experience of losing someone who meant a lot to you. Well, when this

139

happens we start to question God and plead with Him and all sorts of things—and then comes that awful time when you just can't talk to Him any more. This is fairly common and it doesn't mean that God has left you . . . but that you have stepped away from Him slightly. You know He's in control and you know that He's real—but right now, you just can't face Him.

At a time like this, it's important just to acknowledge the Lord's presence. Just say, 'I know you're there Lord, bear with me on this one.' He will understand and He won't let go of you. The danger time comes when we let our grief take control and run away from the Lord altogether; the further we run, the harder it gets to come back . . . and that's backsliding. It's not a laugh, it's a real dilemma and it's a situation you will never ever be happy in. It can eventually lead to turning your back on Jesus . . . but let me stress, this is *very rare*. People think they do it at times, but it's rarely a reality.

We can get into situations at times where we think nobody cares . . . nobody understands and we feel totally alone. And when you think about it—isn't that when you need Jesus more?

Jesus would never give you up without a fight, and as I said, people rarely turn their backs on Him entirely and walk away. So don't confuse this with missing meetings/Bible reading/prayer times . . . God is much bigger than that. It takes a lot more than lack of interest to backslide . . .

14

'I can't explain it to my family!'

Dear Sue,

What do I do if my family are not Christians? They seem to criticise me a lot and sometimes I don't feel as close to them as I used to. How can I show them I care?

In the battle for and against Christian/non-Christian families, the non-Christian family only just loses.

What do I mean? Well, ask any kid from a *Christian* family what it's like and he will tell you that it's hard to come from a house full of churchgoers!

Seeing as they both have problems . . . let's have a look at either side.

The teenager with Christian parents will tell you that he has a lot of pressure on him to go to church, whether he wants to go or not. And like a lot of things . . . the minute you're told you *must* do something, it becomes the only thing you don't want to do. It's a rule . . . do your homework, tidy your room, go to church. If your parents are

141

involved in the running of the youth meeting or any other meeting, then it's doubly hard because you feel you have to support them. What would Mrs So and So think of your mum if you didn't go to communion after she'd spent all that time cutting that bread up into tiny little squares?? If your dad is an elder or a deacon, then the pressure is amazing—especially when you start reading in the Bible about how an elder of the church must have this perfect family and such well-behaved children!

A lot of the time, this kid has trouble finding Jesus for himself. You see, it's all right for you . . . you've become a Christian because you wanted to and you stood up at some great meeting somewhere and went forward and stuff. This kid is not actually sure if he's ever made a decision for Jesus, because in his house it's all anyone ever talks about. A fella we know, called Dave, went to a church for ages and attended the youth meetings, sang in the choir and everything, and everyone just assumed he was a Christian. Dave said it was just so awkward because he knew all the songs, joined in the prayers and every day it became more and more embarrassing to say to someone, 'Actually, I've never made that decision.' It wasn't that he didn't want to, it was just that nobody had ever asked him about it and he was only a young teen and needed someone to approach him.

And it's a very similar situation with Christian families. We know quite a few sons and daughters of leading speakers and evangelists who had never made a commitment to Jesus for themselves until we asked them about it. When you're so closely associated with the 'Christian scene' it's just assumed that you must be part of it.

Also, I think that when you are young, you do need someone to go through your decision with you. It's not impossible for you to make your decision by yourself, but when no one's there to witness it, you sometimes find it more difficult to realise what you've actually done. Which is why the kid with the Christian family would love the opportunity to stand up in an appeal and walk to the front . . . probably like you did. *But*! he had to do that in front of his family, and that's hard, very hard! These are the things that build up a good case for kids going to different churches from their parents.

What??! Yes! I know of plenty of very sensible Christian parents who have said to us, 'I don't mind where he goes to church, I'm just glad that he goes.' Great! This is often an ideal way. There's nothing in the Bible that says we have to like the same kind of meeting as our parents, and if mum and dad go to a more sedate church and all your Christian friends go to the one up the road which caters more for young people . . . then have a chat with your parents about it! They are more than likely to give you the response I've been talking about—and you are more likely to stick with it.

OK. Let's talk about the other side of the fence. You come from a family where you are the only Christian, and your parents, brothers and sisters are not always sympathetic. Well, were you sympathetic to other Christians before you became one yourself? Probably not. So keep that in mind as we talk.

It's a funny thing becoming a Christian . . . if you are not one yourself and your friend all of a sudden puts that one on you, your first reaction can be one of fright. I suppose we read so many things about strange religious sects and hair-raising stories of people who are brainwashed and have all their money taken away from them, that we roll 'religion' into one big ball.

When one of my friends became a Christian, she told me about it while we were standing at the bus stop waiting to come home from work. I was really worried. She told me she had been to a party and met Jesus! Apparently, at this party there was a painting of Jesus on the wall and she went to look at it and this guy came up and asked her if she was interested in meeting Jesus. It was all a bit mixed up, but she said she would and so he prayed with her and she met Him! Well, that's how it sounded to me, and I remember rushing home and telling my mum that one of my friends was well on her way to some kind of breakdown. I was seriously worried about her, she'd obviously been hallucinating . . . maybe this bloke at the party had given her drugs?

I saw her a few times after that, and I spoke to her dad, who was also worried. Apparently she had argued with her dad because his newsagent was open on a Sunday, and she wouldn't eat her food unless everybody said grace. It was alarming! I didn't see her again for months and during that

time, I became a Christian myself. The second
time I went to my church—she was there! I talked
with her and began to realise that she really was a
Christian, that there was nothing wrong with her
apart from an over-enthusiastic desire to tell
everyone else about it! Hopefully it helped
me to restrain myself a bit from walking up to
complete strangers and asking, 'Have you met the
Lord?'

When you first become a Christian, you are
so excited about it that you do tend to go over the
top . . . and that's when family and friends get
worried. Gradually, as they see you calming down
and talking 'normal' again, the pressure is
released.

So, probably when you first became a
Christian, if you looked at it through your parents'
eyes, you would see that they would be very
worried. What is this Christianity? Are they going
to brainwash my daughter? The minister doesn't
even wear a dog-collar! And you . . . you were
probably walking around with your nose in a
Bible, ignoring everyone. You also found yourself
with a whole load of new friends, people from your
church. Well, that's great—but what about your
old friends? Did you give them the elbow? Did
you say to yourself, 'Well, I've asked them if they
want to come to church and they don't'?

Our heads get turned. Same as with a lot of
things really—we get a new boyfriend/girlfriend
and everyone else seems irrelevant. A new youth
club starts up, the only people that matter to you
any more are the ones who go to it. Homework

suffers 'cos you're trying to get it done to get to the club. Your friend needs to stay in—do you stay in with her? . . . No way, the club's open, sorry.

Becoming a Christian shouldn't mean ignoring everything else. Life still goes on. Your friends still need you, your family still want you and there's still school to go to.

So this is what you need to do:

1. Sort out which meetings at church are the most important for you at this moment.
2. Spend at least one evening a week with your non-Christian friends.
3. Spend another evening indoors with your family. Not upstairs in your room, but downstairs where they can be with you.
4. Leave plenty of time for homework, chores around the house and other normal things.

You will never impress your mum and dad by carrying a Bible round the house and quoting verses at them. They will not admire your dedication in how many times a week you are 'up that church again'. The only way they will see that Christianity works, is when they see it in your life! It's true! At the moment, church is like a rival. It's the thing that keeps you out of the house all week.

For your friends, it's the thing that's taken you away from them. It's the enemy! They need to see that you are still you, but you care a little bit more, that you listen when they tell you things.

Fine, pray for your friends when you are on your own with the Lord . . . but don't shove it in their faces. They are bewildered, they don't understand . . . and you know what happens when you don't understand something??? You laugh at it! It doesn't make it go away, but it makes you feel better . . . that's why sometimes people laugh at you when you say you're going to church. It's not because they are mocking you . . . it's because they don't understand it, it's foreign to them, they're uncomfortable.

Please go easy on your family. They are having a hard time coming to terms with your new-found faith. They will tease, and sing 'Hallelujah' at you now and again. Try and have the guts to laugh with them.

When Jesus was dying in agony on the cross for you and your family, He said, 'Father, forgive them, they don't know what they're doing.' You are only receiving some gentle teasing. I think you should be able to swallow hard and try to understand.

Last thing . . . If you really want to impress your family about how this Christianity thing works . . . then . . . Tidy Up Your Room!! Hah! Make Them A Cup Of Tea Without Being Asked! Hah! Offer To Help! Am I getting through?

I do understand that it's difficult for you, but believe me John and I have met many many kids like you who have gradually brought their whole families (aunts and uncles too!) to the Lord. It is entirely possible, but it's up to you. Slow down, be gentle, pray for them and live as Jesus would want you to.

15

'What is "communion" . . . really?'

Dear Sue,

I've been taking communion for three months now, but I'm ashamed to say that I still don't really understand what it's about. Please could you explain it?

I wish more people had the nerve to admit when they don't understand things! I know I do it myself—in a shop with some bloke explaining how this new word processor works, I'm standing there nodding vigorously and he really thinks I know what he's talking about! The worse thing then, is when they ask you something . . . 'So has your old computer got a mouse?' 'Er . . . I . . . er . . . well, I had a hamster once . . .'

I think, with communion, a lot of people start taking it because someone comes along and pushes a piece of bread under their nose and they feel it would be impolite to refuse it. Refusing the bread gives everyone else one of two impressions. One, you are not a Christian (tut tut . . .), or two, you have had a blazing row with someone and you've not had time to make amends before the

149

service. This is the most interesting one because you can look round and find out who else isn't taking it—and *then* you've sussed out who they've rowed with!)

These are the most common reasons for people *not* taking communion. However, there are several reasons why people *do* take it. The first is because they understand what it's all about and the second is because they *don't* understand what it's all about!

The nice thing about communion is that it's the only service we are actually commanded to go to. Obviously in the time of Paul, communion was quite a feast and something that you wouldn't miss for the world. Unfortunately, we tend to play it down a bit in our churches these days, which is quite a shame. We've been to a few really nice communions where the church members have sat around very informally and passed a loaf round, whilst chatting to each other about things God has done for them, and it's very much a social event. That's what 'meeting together' is all about!

Communion is a kind of social gathering/remembrance service and although part of it is remembering Jesus' death, it's also partly a celebration. When you see Remembrance Services on TV, although they have a sombre tone (remembering soldiers who have given their lives in war), when you see the razzmatazz they put on at the Albert Hall and places, it's hardly quiet, is it? And communion's the same, we are celebrating a death!

OK. So first you really have to get to grips with why Jesus' death was so important, and believe me, an awful lot of folk don't understand this bit . . .

In one way I suppose it's a bit gory—but then there wasn't anything particularly pleasant about dying. On the other hand, as I said, Jesus' death was a celebration, which was why Jesus shouted in great victory, 'It is finished!' He died on a high note.

So *what* was finished?

We often tend to think that it was as if Jesus was saying, 'Hooray—I'm finally dead!' . . . well, think about it, would you be thrilled if someone you loved said to you, 'I love you so much that I'm going to prove it by chucking myself off a bridge'? Of course you wouldn't be thrilled, you'd be devastated and that's what brings me to say that there was much more to Jesus' death than just dying to show how much He loved you!

Now bear with me, because I'm going to have to take you back to the Old Testament times—don't you dare switch off, we've come this far and you are very near to discovering the absolute reason why Jesus died. Right?

In Old Testament times the Jews had a great festival called the Feast of the Passover. It was the day in their year when all their sins were forgiven. It used to happen like this:

The feast of the Passover always started with the search for an innocent animal. They had to find one without any kind of spot or blemish—it had to be as pure as possible. Once they had found such an animal, they had to kill it. (No, I don't like that bit either, but then death has never been nice.) But you see, the only way the Jews

151

could get forgiveness for their sins was to spill
blood. God had demanded that sin was payable
by death. You could only rid yourself of sin by
bringing to God the blood of innocence, and
because no man was completely innocent, an
animal had to be found.

Now, when this blood had been collected it
would be taken by the High Priest into a place
called the Holy of Holies . . . it was like a mega-
holy part of the temple that only the High Priest
was allowed to enter. Inside this place there would
have been quite a strange sight. There was a box,
called the Ark of the Covenant and inside the box
were some strange objects. There was Aaron's rod
(the one that grew and budded), there was a pot of
manna (from the days in the wilderness) and there
were the ten commandments.

On top of the box were two statues of angel-
like creatures called the Cherubim—they stood for
the holiness and justice of God. (This is getting to
sound like a video game . . . !)

Now, the Cherubim were placed so that they
looked down onto the contents of this box. If you
were to look down in the same position you would
realise that all the Cherubim could see was the
failure of man.

Think about it!

1. Aaron's rod . . . This was supposed
   to be a symbol of God's leadership.
   The staff held in the hand of the
   man of God and yet the people had
   moaned and said, 'We don't want

him to lead us . . . we want
someone else!'
2. The pot of manna . . . representing
God's provision. When the children
of Israel were wandering around in
the wilderness God gave them food
in the form of manna. Were they
happy about this? No, they got
bored and wanted meat to eat, they
didn't want God's provision.
3. The ten commandments . . . God's
laws which were broken within five
minutes of them being given.

Failure. Sin. Wrongdoing . . . call it what you
like, the Cherubim had to sit and look at it for 364
days of the year. Then for just that one day of the
year, the Jews would celebrate because the High
Priest would enter this Holy Place and sprinkle
this innocent blood all over the box (the Ark of the
Covenant). So for just that one day, all the
Cherubim could see was the blood of an innocent
animal—they couldn't see the sin any more . . .
and that meant that God was looking at the
innocent blood too. So God was able to forgive the
sin, wipe it clean from the slate, because He saw
the blood instead. The sin was covered by the
blood. (Now you're beginning to recall the old
hymn words, aren't you?)
So it was a great day for the Jews, their sins
were forgiven and they could rejoice. But by the
end of the day they would understand that it
would be whole year before it would happen again.

The High Priest would come out of the Holy of Holies, and life would go on.

I hope you're still with me because that's the difficult bit out of the way, and maybe you can start to see a picture forming in your mind of what happened next.

The system with the High Priest was obviously not good enough, and God knew that the only way sins would be forgiven for ever was if a pure, unblemished, innocent man were to be killed instead. The only problem was, of course, there was no such person on the face of the earth. Only one person was without sin and that person was God. The three persons of God had to come into action. The Father, the Son and the Holy Spirit had work to do. The Father, the all-powerful force behind creation, had to send the Son, God in the form of a human being, to be killed in our place.

Jesus was then born as a baby and lived an innocent life so that when the time was right, He would be crucified until He died.

Let me tell you what happened when Jesus died. It wasn't quite as easy as killing an animal. When Jesus died it was as if God stood at one end of the universe and rolled every sin that had ever been committed into a huge ball the size of a world. This ball was made up of every sin that you and I had ever committed, any sin we are committing at this moment, and any sin we might commit in the future. And then while Jesus hung in pain on the cross, God the Father stood at the other end of the universe and took that ball of fire in His huge hands and flung it with all His might, power and wrath . . . at Jesus. The full impact of the sins of the world hit Jesus squarely where He was hanging. And that's when Jesus cried, 'It is finished.' He died and took His blood up to heaven and, looking down (like the Cherubim did), could sprinkle His blood over the world. So God saw just the blood of Jesus covering our sin.

Now the thing is, Jesus never left the presence of God. If you remember, the High Priest had to come out of the Holy of Holies and so let the people down until a year later. But Jesus stayed in the presence of God for ever, and He's still there covering you with His blood and forgiving you for your sin . . . if you believe in Him. And because Jesus stayed where He was, He sent the third part of the Trinity, the Holy Spirit, down to earth as a helper and comforter.

Phew! I know that's rather a long story, but it's the best way I can explain to you the significance of Jesus' death, so now I can finish off explaining to you about communion. If you look in Luke chapter 22, you'll see that the Last Supper happened on the day called the Passover. Jesus chose this day so that His disciples would hopefully see the significance of what He was about to do. When He picked up the bread they were about to eat, He tore it and then shared it round, and while He was doing this He likened the loaf to His own body, saying that He too was going to be torn apart. I don't know how much the disciples took in at the time, but Jesus said to them, 'This is my body given for you, do this in remembrance of me.' Then He did the same thing with the wine, asking them to share it but reminding them that when they drank wine like this in future they should remember that the blood of Jesus was the 'new covenant'—in other words the new promise (unlike the Old Testament way)— and they should remember how Jesus gave His own blood to forgive their sins.

So these days when we take communion, that's what we are doing! We are remembering that first time when Jesus got together with His disciples and explained how He would die. When we are offered bread, it's the same as when Jesus offered it, it's to remember that His body was broken for you. Then again the wine comes round and we remember that the innocent animal wasn't enough, it took Jesus' blood to take away our sins for ever.

Hopefully you can now see why communion is important. It's a very special time . . . not so much a service as a time of fellowship, sharing with each other. There is no point in taking communion if you are not fully convinced that you are a Christian and that Jesus died for you.

Better now? Things make so much more sense once you know why you're doing them, don't they?

16

'What's in it for me?'

Dear Sue,

This is going to sound very selfish, I know, but what exactly do I get from becoming a Christian?

I know what you mean, it does sound selfish, but on the other hand it's a fairly sensible thing to want to know. These days nobody does anything until they find out what's in it for them, and it's a question you are liable to be asked as a Christian quite often.

John and I used to do this sketch which we called 'the Ronnie and Eric Sketch'. It was all about two fellas meeting in the pub like they usually do, for a quiet pint at lunch time. But this time there was something different. This time when they met, Ronnie had become a Christian and he was very determined to tell Eric all about it. So for ages he tries to butt in to the conversation with the fact that he's become a Christian and he finds it much harder work than he first thought. After a very slow start, where he keeps mumbling, 'Er . . . I've er . . . I've become . . . er . . . I've become a er . . . '

Eric starts to get very frustrated trying to guess *what* he has become! 'You've become a

157

what, Ron? Boy scout? . . . postman? . . . nun?
. . . *what*?' Then, fearing the worst of his best
friend, he gasps, ' . . . 'ere, you're not a . . . ?'

Ronnie calms him down and says, 'No, no
Eric. I've become a Christian.'

From here on, Ronnie tries to explain what
it's like to be a Christian, and what the benefits
are. He goes through the fact that it's a very
happy church where everyone sings joyfully and
claps their hands. He tells him about the fact that
Christians don't just wear black boring clothes
these days—in fact they wear whatever they like!
He sings the praises of the family feeling in the
meetings and the wonderful music that the
worship band play.

In fact he harps on for quite a while and
suggests that Eric might like to try his church
himself some time. With that he gets up and
starts to leave the pub. Eric shouts after him
'Going down the church for a sing-song, eh, Ron?'

'Yeah, that's right,' smiles Ronnie
apologetically.

Eric is left sitting on his own at the table
and he turns to the audience with a quizzical look
on his face and says, 'That's funny. I always
thought it had something to do with Jesus.'

And that's the thing, isn't it? When we tell
our friends that we're Christians, we do tend to go
on about all the things we do at church that we
think they'll like.

When I was first looking for God, I remember
going to a church and waiting for all the singing
and stuff to be over because I wanted to hear what
the minister was going to say. I had decided that

he was the key to me finding out if there really was a Jesus—and it seemed an age while the congregation went through all this other stuff. My job at the time was working with rock stars, so if I wanted music I went to work. If I wanted Jesus, it stood to reason that I had to go to a church.

So what's so important about being a Christian? I can sing and dance at a rave, I can get a close family feeling at home . . . what's it going to do for me?

Let's talk about Eternity. A lot of people view eternity as something that happens after you die. It's a long, long time—sort of for ever really. On the other hand, Double English at school can also be termed an eternity, can't it? The hour you have to sit on a settee and be nice to an aunt you haven't seen for fifty million years can seem like eternity too, right?

Someone once said to me that to figure out what eternity's about . . . imagine an eagle soaring round the top of a mountain, and once every thousand years it touches the tip of the mountain with its wing. By the time that eagle has worn that mountain to the ground . . . *eternity will have only just begun!* Devastating, isn't it??

So what we're talking about here is your life going on for *that* kind of eternity. And it doesn't start after you die, it's already started now! So it's important that you sort out how you want to spend this inconceivable amount of time. You have two choices—you can spend it with God or without Him. While you are considering this, you should also consider the fact that eternity is an awfully long time to be wrong! So one of the things you get out of it is a nice place to spend the rest of your life!

But as I said, it doesn't start after you die . . . it starts now! Jesus has a lot to offer you and we'll go through that in a minute, but first you really do need to consider all sorts of painful things. For instance, you have no guarantee how long your life span on earth will be. I don't like talking about death and things, but it is a fact of life! I'm not trying to give you a 'What if you fall under a bus tomorrow and don't know Jesus' sort of lecture—but all the same you can't even guarantee your next breath!

People die in so many different ways. A friend was telling me of an old man she visited in hospital. She had been told he was dying and he was very frail. For days when she visited him, he never said a word and he just lay there with a huge tear in one of his eyes. She said it was the most sorry sight she'd ever seen. On the day he died, she was there and she described it like this: 'He just closed his eyes and the tear rolled right down his face.' I found that description immensely sad . . . but what about this one??

A man was reported in the papers as having had a heart attack while watching his favourite comedians on the telly. He laughed so hard that it brought on the heart attack and he died sitting in his armchair in front of the TV! . . . Now, here we have two totally different ways of 'meeting your Maker'. But we have no way of knowing where they went! Somehow you assume that the sad man went to hell and the happy man went to heaven . . . or maybe the sad man went to heaven to be comforted and the happy man went to hell for laughing at rude jokes! Maybe they both went to hell . . . the only thing we can be sure of is that they both went *somewhere*!

The Bible has never stated that if you become a Christian, life will automatically become perfect, but it does say that if you believe in Jesus, you will spend eternity with Him in heaven. Now, don't let anyone convince you that heaven is a dull place where people play harps all day and that hell is a constant rave. Listen! *Heaven is where the party is!*

You can't chose *when* to go but you can chose *where* to go! People are always saying, 'I'll wait until I'm older.' But you really don't have that kind of choice. Right now you have to make up your mind what kind of life you want to lead. Is it to be God-centred or Self-centred? That's the choice, and until you make any decision at all, then your life will always be Self-centred.

So let's look at Self-centred. My sister Jeannie married a bloke called Graham who was fairly high up in the TV world. So at the wedding there were some guests from 'the business'. At the reception, this producer came up to John and me and said, 'I really enjoyed the wedding service. It was wonderful to see a proper Christian wedding—but I find some of the words of the hymns very hard to swallow.'

We were rather surprised to hear him talking about Christian things, but decided to take him up on his query.

'What words were they?' we asked in unison.

'Well, in the hymn "When I survey the wondrous cross" it says "Forbid it Lord that I should boast, save in the death of Christ my Lord." '

Still a bit confused, we waited. He shrugged his shoulders and said, 'I've made some extremely good programmes for TV. I've been nominated for awards, and I really don't see why I can't boast about them. What's wrong with being proud of doing a good job?'

Isn't it strange, the things that keep people away from God? I suppose when your life is Self-centred, you are quite protective of it. You need people to admire your work and say 'Well done' now and again, and you see, there's nothing wrong with that! It is not wrong to feel satisfied when you've done something good.

It's just the place you give it in your life that can be wrong.

So why put Jesus first? Why give Him a place in your life? When God created the world He thought it was such a brilliant place that He couldn't wait to create you to live on it. You are perfectly made for this planet and all the good things on it, and above all God wants you to enjoy His creation—and that includes fun and laughter, as well as environmentally friendly things! He created *sound, smell, sight, feelings, colour* . . . you name it! The idea was that we use it for good. Unfortunately, things go wrong and the devil has done his best to destroy and pervert those things that were pure. So now you can *listen* to funny jokes or dirty jokes, you can *smell* flowers or glue, you can *watch* a baby being born or a video nasty, you can *feel* love or hate, and you can reject *black* or *white*.

God gave us the choice. We could trust that He had good things in mind for us or we could do our own thing. Now, deep down I think most of us want to do right and we want to succeed. (That's why we like people to say 'well done'.) And to prove this point, we are forever getting a 'guilty conscience', aren't we? The worst feeling in the world is when you do something badly wrong and no matter what you do, you can't put it right and it makes you feel absolutely awful. Example? You get out of the wrong side of bed and go to school in a bad mood. When you get there, your friend says to you, 'I bought this jacket with my birthday money . . . what d'you think?'

And because you're not in the mood to be jolly, you say, 'S'all right.' In actual fact, it's a brilliant jacket and you'd love one like it, so you're jealous as well as moody. Your friend feels as if someone's smacked her in the mouth and she looks terribly disappointed. Later on in the day you realise you've been mean and try to make it up. By now your friend has decided you're not worth knowing and she's gone off with someone else. You know how it is!

In actual fact it's quite a small problem if you compare it with murdering someone . . . but they both leave you with a nasty taste in your mouth and a twisted feeling in your stomach that you've just done something you can't undo. OK. Now listen to this . . .

> *Their sins and the evil things they do—*
> *I will not remember any more.*
> (Hebrews 10:17)

> *Let us come near to God with a sincere heart and a sure faith, because **we have been made free from a guilty conscience** . . . Let us hold firmly to the hope that we have confessed, because **we can trust God to do what he promised.***
> (Hebrews 10:22–23, my emphasis)

So here is something that you get out of becoming a Christian. Jesus is there to take the punishment for all the stupid things you've ever said or done. Whether it's little things (like with the jacket) or bigger things like stealing or sleeping with someone. Ouch! Sorry, did I tread on your toes just then?

It cost Jesus everything to take that punishment—He even lost contact with His Father who couldn't look at the sin Jesus was carrying on the cross. But before Jesus took that sin . . . God couldn't bear to look at *you*!

So you've gained a friend in God the Father and Creator of the world, *plus* the freedom of living without the weight of sin on your back all the time. That's why the hymn-writer wrote, 'What a friend we have in Jesus, all our sins and griefs to bear.'

Yes, and the next line of that hymn goes 'What a privilege to carry everything to God in prayer.'

So here's your next advantage. Someone to talk to. Someone like you've never had before. Those of us with good friends know what it's like to share secrets and talk over crisis problems with them. But if you are honest, you would admit that there are some things that you wouldn't even tell *them*!

There are times in everyone's life when you all of a sudden have this terrible fear that you are abnormal in some way. You see someone with a perfect figure and then look at your own! . . . Some lumps are too big, some haven't even budged since you were three years old . . . are you weird or what?? Maybe you hear of some terrible disease and you start to imagine the symptoms in your own body. It can be terrifying, and there's no way you're going to talk to anyone about it, because you're too frightened. You can tell Jesus about it. He's not going to tell anyone else and He will listen for as long as you want to talk. He will answer too! Maybe not always in the way you expect, but He will answer.

Talking to God is a great hobby! I often talk things over with the Lord as I'm walking about. Sometimes He will send someone to help with the problem, sometimes I will find the answer in my next Bible reading and sometimes just talking it through with someone who is so holy and just, makes you realise that it's a case of doing right or wrong. Look up the chapter of prayer if you're still confused.

So having Jesus in your life is a great big plus. It's good to know Jesus can heal bodies, and broken hearts. It's great to realise that heaven has a place marked out for you, but the *real* advantage of being a Christian is *knowing* God personally.

> *Oh what peace we often forfeit.*
> *Oh what needless pain we bear.*
> *All because we do not carry*
> *Everything to God in prayer.*

17

'What's the difference?'

Dear Sue,

I always get into such a mess at school when people ask me why I believe in God. We have a very mixed school and there's lots of different religions. . . so how do I make Christianity sound better than the others?

First of all, congratulations on being in a position where people are asking you about your faith! I have so many teenagers writing to me to ask how to go about introducing Christianity into their conversation, so it's great to hear from someone who already has!

I wonder what your friends think of when they talk about God? What does He look like? How does He act towards you? When we talk about 'God' we kind of pigeon-hole Him into this universal picture seen in film and pantomimes. So then when someone says 'I believe in God' or 'I don't believe in God' . . . it's always interesting to ask them what kind of God they do or don't believe in! You'll get a wonderful selection of descriptions, including the usual one of a huge man who sits on a fluffy cloud and looks down on you from a great height. He usually has a long flowing white beard to go with his long flowing white coat and he has lightning coming out of his fingertips. In fact if you put a long *red* coat on him . . . he could easily pass for Father Christmas— same type of job: being a father-figure and giving out presents to people whilst lovingly 'ho ho ho'ing at them!

Others will see God as a force (à la Star Wars) who doesn't so much have lightning coming out of his fingers, as *is* the lightning itself—a kind of fluorescent electric current thing that flies around the universe saving people from a fate worse than Darth Vader.

So then it's important that you explain what *your* God is like. The fact that He is a real person, a father and a spirit is a bit mind-blowing, so it's probably better to concentrate on Jesus being made in the likeness of God, so that you can describe Him as a personal God, someone you can get to know.

The reason that the personal side is important, is that this is where other religions fail. They have no personal God, and even when they have something along those lines, he's a God who punishes and not a God who loves.

You see, most religions are based around the same thing. They are all trying to please their God. If they do enough religious things (chants, prayers, etc.) and then enough good deeds (being kind to people, etc.) they will finally, one great day, get to meet their God. On the other hand, if they don't behave themselves, their God is likely to punish them . . . and then they have to work their way back into his favour all over again. So life for most religions is a series of punishments and penances. That's why you will hear some pop stars sing about religion. Madonna and the Pet Shop Boys, for instance, were brought up very religiously and were never told of God's love—only His punishment. Hence the worrying lyrics of some of their songs (Papa Don't Preach/It's A Sin . . . etc.).

Working your way up to God is a long long climb, and actually totally impossible, but everyone's searching for a way back. Christianity is different. We don't go searching for God, trying to seek His favour and showing Him how good we are.

God came looking for us. He died to show us how bad we were! God came down to earth in the form of Jesus—He became like us, so that He could experience the kind of life we had. He was different, in that He didn't sin and then He gave His life up for us. If you like, God climbed down the ladder and gave us His hand. With all other religions, the people have to try and climb a ladder up to their God who is sitting somewhere totally unattainable.

So the personal experience is probably the biggest difference that you could talk to your friends about. The other thing that always makes a difference is your own testimony. It's your story of how you became a Christian, and whatever arguments your friends might have— they can't deny your own story without branding you a liar!

Don't go on the defensive too much. Try to share your story as genuinely and simply as you can, and don't be afraid to say 'I don't know' if you can't answer their questions. People appreciate that a lot more than some smart-alec answer. (and you can always go away and try to find the answer to their question if you think it's important!) I hope you have a lot of fun talking to your schoolmates about your best friend. I wonder if they can say that *their* God is their best friend too?

18

'Why do people get killed?'

> Dear Sue,
>
> I can't understand why people get killed if there's a God. Why doesn't He stop it?

I can never understand why people always blame God for everything that goes wrong! Do you know, I've heard God blamed for everything from exam failures to earthquakes! Most of the time the moans come from people who 'don't believe in God' . . . but as I said, He certainly gets blamed a lot for someone who doesn't exist! It's a shame so many folk use God as a cop-out. Have you ever noticed that if there's a bad snowstorm and someone is killed . . . it's God's fault? If someone comes into extreme wealth or has a miraculous escape from a car accident then it's 'lucky' . . . nothing to do with God at all this time! God gets the blame but none of the credit. So did God get it wrong?

The obvious answer is that as well as there being a God there's also a devil. The devil likes to corrupt and steal the thunder and the Bible refers to him as 'prowling around like a roaring lion'.

Much of the bad in the world comes from him directly. We don't help much, because we give him so much ammunition at times. We lose our tempers when we could have sorted something out amicably, we stop speaking to someone out of spite when it would have been better to sit and talk it over.

And then we kill people. Yes, this is the big issue. God doesn't kill people . . . people kill people. It was never God's desire that we should be at war with one another. It wasn't God that sowed a seed of jealousy in our hearts that made us murder and destroy. How can we possibly blame God for those things? When Adam and Eve first sinned in the Garden of Eden, bad things entered the world. Weeds began to grow and choke the beautiful plants that God had made. Not only did Adam and Eve start to go bad, but the whole of creation started to go bad.

These days we have great evidence of just how bad things have got. Every other charity is trying to do something about it—'Save the Whales', 'Save the Trees', 'People Against Aids', 'Life not Abortion'. We're in a right state.

If we had followed God's law from the beginning none of this would have happened! But God gave us a choice, just as He gave Adam and Eve a choice. Obey or disobey . . . and suffer the consequences. So really, an awful lot of the things that are wrong with our world, are actually our fault! This is not just a theory supported by Christians . . . this is a worldwide statement! All of a sudden we have been brought up with a start,

172

as we see our planet going rotten in front of our eyes.

Michael Jackson sings a brilliant song called 'The Man in the Mirror'. It goes like this:

> I'm starting with the man in the mirror.
> I'm asking him to change his ways.
> I'm starting with the man in the mirror.
> If you wanna make the world a better place
> Take a look at yourself and make a change.

God made us a wonderful world . . . We chose to destroy it.

19

'I can't smile ALL the time!'

Dear Sue,

My face is cracking! People keep telling me that because I'm a Christian, I should be constantly happy . . . Is this true? I don't think I can grin and bear it much longer!

Cheer up! It's not that bad! (ooops sorry . . .) You mean to say that you are not incredibly happy every moment of your life?? Strange, isn't it, the ideas people have of what a Christian is. I can't honestly say that the Bible teaches us to be constantly happy . . . it certainly says we should have 'life' in all its fullness, but if you asked folk what that meant to them, you'd get a lot of different answers. I suppose a mountain climber could tell you he's lived life to the full, but he'd certainly have a few hairy adventures to his name! A mother with a family who have grown up beautifully would probably say she's lived her life to the full . . . but I bet she had a few ding-dongs with them on the way!

To 'live life to the full', you've got to have experienced pain and heartache, you've got to go through rough times . . . but you come out rejoicing, you come out the other end!

Let me tell you a kind of funny story . . . A couple of years ago we were offered a tour of America. We were going for six weeks and obviously we were looking forward to it. We had to apply for a visa. (You still needed them, even for a holiday, until two years ago.) It was just a formality and loads of our friends had been over to the States to other churches and things. So, we were rather put out when we received a compliment slip with a curt 'we have rejected your application' stamped on it. As this was obviously a mistake, we sent our passports off again . . . and the same thing happened. We couldn't understand what was going on so we went to a travel agency and asked them to apply for a visa for us. A few days later back it came again! By now, our passport was beginning to look decidedly shady with all these refusals stamped in it. We were still mystified as to why this was happening, so we wrote to the American Embassy and explained that we were a Christian band, and that we would be touring around youth groups, and that our expenses were going to be paid, etc., etc., and *still* our passports came back . . . NO!

By now we were beginning to think that our dark and distant past had something to do with spies and things, so we decided to speak to them personally. We were granted an interview, and duly arrived at the American Embassy after being scrutinised by the guards and having our

176

passports whipped away from us. After four hours of queuing from one desk to another, we finally found ourselves sitting opposite a lady who had the answers to all our problems.

What she said to us will live with us for ever, and I must admit it shocked us into laughter . . .

She said, 'I think I'm a good judge of character, and I can tell just by looking at you, that you two are much too happy and carefree. Your lifestyle is very laid-back and you enjoy what you do. Therefore I'm refusing your application for a visa to America.'

'Stunned' was an inappropriate word for how we felt. Eventually I said to her, 'Do you actually mean you're turning down our visa because we're *too happy*?!'

She looked at us very solemnly and said, 'Yes.'

We both gasped, fell back in our chairs and laughed. We just couldn't believe it! Too happy? We asked her to explain how being too happy could keep you out of America.

'Your lifestyle takes you from town to town, you have an extensive itinerary and I think if we let you into America, you would not come back. You would settle there and become illegal immigrants.'

This was all so ludicrous we were speechless!

'But we have nearly a year's work booked up in this country . . . we *have* to come back to fulfil our bookings!'

No reply.

177

'We don't want to live in America . . . we like it here!' (Probably not a good answer!)

We were then asked to produce the deeds of our house (the kind of thing everyone carries around in their pocket . . .) and letters of recommendation.

We went home and arranged for tons of letters of recommendation from every influential person we knew, we had the deeds of our house photostatted by our building society . . . (Our house is very old, and the deeds were over a hundred pages long!)

Did we succeed? Did we get our visa?

Not only did we not get it, but we were told not even to try to go to America *on holiday* for at least two years!

This story still astounds us now—and all because we were too happy!!

So let this be a warning to happy Christians everywhere!! When it comes to being happy, John and I are experts on the matter!

There's no doubt that God wants you to be happy and wants you to enjoy His creation, but I don't think the idea has ever been that you lie back and let God get on with it.

You are *His* servant . . . not the other way round! Things will go wrong in your life and it's *then* that you show the confidence you have in God. It's much more than happiness, it's assurance that God has your life in hand, and He knows what He's doing. That's why, at times, you get these 'grinny' Christians who are always telling you 'Be of good cheer' . . . it's not enough, is it? There's a great Peanuts cartoon of Snoopy sitting

in the freezing cold . . . he's got icicles on his fur
and his teeth are chattering. Along come Lucy and
her friends, they see Snoopy and say to each
other, 'Ah! Look at poor old Snoopy, he looks
terrible. Let's do something to help.' And they run
over to him and pat him on his freezing fur and
say, 'Be of good cheer, Snoopy, be of good cheer.'
And then they push off!

Now, for Snoopy to 'be of good cheer' he
needed more than a word of encouragement, he
needed someone to put a blanket round him and
toast him his favourite marshmallows! There's
more to being a happy Christian than quoting
Bible verses at people!

So really, a Christian should be someone
who makes the people *surrounding* him smile,
more than just smiling himself. Maybe you can
only do a little, maybe you can do a lot. The lady
who sent a postcard to Terry Waite in prison
probably thought she wasn't doing much, but boy!
it did Terry Waite good, didn't it?

20

'Tell me there's a heaven . . .'

Dear Sue,

I have a lot of questions about dying and heaven and hell and stuff like that. I know it's a bit morbid, but I don't know who else to ask.

OK, let's tackle this head on. Most people of your age have known someone who has died. It might have been someone close, it might have been someone in another class at school. Either way it brings up all sorts of questions in your head that were never there before. I don't think there's anything like the realisation that whatever you do, you can't bring that person back. It's so weird, isn't it? One day you're chatting away to someone and the next day you will never see them again in this life. All of a sudden, God and Heaven and Hell and Life are more important to you than anything else. Suddenly life isn't a game any more, everything is real.

Death affects everyone differently—that's OK, you have to work it out your way. In the last couple of years, John and I have worked at four schools where a death has occurred while we've been there or a few days before we've arrived. Two were accidents, one was a hit-and-run right outside the school and one was a suicide. We've watched the reaction of the pupils. Some kids immediately cry as the accident is announced in assembly, most of them look down at the floor and a few fidget and try to get the attraction of the kid next to them for a laugh. All of those reactions are fine—as I said, you have to handle it your way.

We were playing in a school on the day of a funeral. Around sixty of the pupils were going to the funeral of a young boy from their school. It was hard for us, especially as these young teenagers were walking around the school dressed in black and looking terrified at the thought of the service they were about to go to. The teachers asked us to carry on with some music lessons, so we did. We told the kids to join in the lesson only if they felt they could, and if not we wouldn't worry them. I asked for a volunteer to come out and have a go at my synthesiser . . . as usual there were quite a few hands. I chose a lad who had a riot of a time pressing all the keys and playing tunes with weird noises coming out. The other kids cheered him . . . and I thought to myself, 'Great! maybe it's not going to be such a difficult class after all.'

After the lesson (which had included around a hundred kids), three teachers came up to thank us and to express their amazement that the boy who had played the synthesiser was the brother of the boy who had died . . . just for a few minutes there, he had his mind taken off the tragedy, and the teachers were so pleased.

Some kids laugh and make cruel jokes when someone dies. There is always an influx of jokes in school after a disaster . . . we've had Lockerbie jokes, Freddie Mercury jokes, Ethiopian jokes, IRA jokes. Why? Because it's frightening and we think if we laugh it off, maybe we can forget it. There's a saying that if you throw a stone into a crowd of dogs, the dog that yelps the loudest is the one that got hit. And we are the same. When we get hit by something (like the death of someone we know) we yelp very loudly indeed!

When Jesus died He said, 'Father forgive them, they don't know what they're doing.' And in a small way, it's the same for us when we react to a death—we don't know what we're doing.

For ourselves, I guess we fear dying because there's pain involved. But when other people die, the fear is different, it's the fear of not knowing where they've gone, what's happened to them, will I see them again?

For a while you can kid yourself that your friend has gone on holiday . . . you can keep that up for weeks. But as time passes by, you reach for the phone because there's this film on TV that you know your friend will love . . . and you get halfway through dialling the number before you realise what you're doing.

When my mum died, there were so many little infuriating things that I couldn't do any more. I still don't know how long to cook certain dishes, because I always relied on phoning my mum to ask. I wanted so much to tell her that Princess Diana had done a walkabout in our town, because she was a great fan of Diana, and I wanted to go home and rush to the phone and tell her what she was wearing . . . They're very small things, but they last for ever. I can never share these things with my mum.

So what is our hope? Is there really a place called heaven? Will we meet again?

The Bible gives us every reason to believe that this is so. One of the reasons Jesus died was to prove to us that there is a life after you've died. He came back and showed the disciples His body. 'Touch me', He said. He was a real person made of flesh and blood; He wasn't a ghost or anything like that. When Thomas touched His side, his hand didn't go straight through Him! Jesus sat down and *ate a meal* with His friends . . . you'd have a job doing that with no body wouldn't you?! Jesus died, went to heaven where His Father was, and then appeared to over three hundred people to prove that He was alive once more.

So I don't think you have to worry over whether there is a heaven or not . . . just whether you're going there (but that's another chapter!) It would be hard to explain where heaven is, because as far as I can make out it's in a different dimension. Jesus 'appeared' to the disciples in a room, He didn't walk through the door—He just appeared out of nowhere, which was why the disciples were so afraid and thought He was a ghost! I think it's safe to say that heaven and hell are not 'up and down', but there again it's safe to say that one is an extremely good place to be—and the other one you wouldn't wanna be seen dead in, OK?

There are several very popular questions regarding life after death. Probably the most popular is, 'Will I recognise people I have known in this life?'

Sure! Although we will have a new body, people still recognised Jesus when He appeared to them, and I think the same will go for you and your friends and relations. If they are there you will recognise them. I said in one of the other chapters that heaven is where the party is—and it's true! Heaven is a place of celebration, but that doesn't mean you'll be singing choruses all day long. It's more a celebration because heaven will be as it should be, no more pain, suffering, jealousy, fear . . . it just won't exist! And the beauty of it is—you'll still like yourself in the morning! No guilty hangovers from the night before!

Hell, on the other hand is best explained by saying that it's a place where God isn't—if you can imagine a world where there is no love, no compassion, no laughter and nothing to soothe your worried mind. I heard someone say just the other day that it's no good shrugging your shoulders and saying, 'Well at least I'll be with my mates' . . . because there is no grace in hell, therefore no one would be a friend to anyone else. I think that's a terrible thought, being in agony, frightened and not having anyone to share your fears with.

I believe that the best of God's creation will be in heaven and that includes animals. I'm afraid that animals in this world do not have souls, and therefore when they die, that's it. I know that's sad because we who love animals miss them dearly when they die. But I think you'll find that heaven will have animals. It's a place where the lion will lie down with the lamb, and I for one am looking forward to that day tremendously! I would absolutely love to stroke a tiger, wouldn't you?

Boy, we've certainly gone through a few topics here and we've come a long way from the beginning of the letter.

So, summing up what we've been talking about . . . when death hits a member of your family or friends, then you must grieve however you see fit. Remember, some people cry, some become almost hysterical with laughter, some get extremely angry with God (that's OK, He understands) and some don't seem to react at all.

Please can I just say to you, that if you are in this position, it is very important to react eventually. Please don't be afraid to let your feelings out. My doctor once told my sister that the best advice he could give her to help unwind stress, was to go to a jumble sale, buy up a load of old crockery, go out into the garden and smash the lot! Sometimes that's what we feel we would like to do. It's OK. God does understand and because of this it is very important not to leave Him out of it.

It doesn't matter if all you can say is 'Lord, I just don't know how to talk to You at the moment, but I'm glad You're there.' Just acknowledge Him. There's a verse, isn't there?

> *'Remember the Lord in all you do,*
> *and he will give you success.'*
>   (Proverbs 3:6).

The Bible has all the best advice.